D0142931

HONORING *the* ANCESTORS

••• HONORING
the ANCESTORS

An African Cultural
Interpretation of
Black Religion
and Literature

DONALD H. MATTHEWS

New York • Oxford

Oxford University Press

1998

ALBRIGHT COLLEGE LIBRARY

Oxford University Press

Oxford   New York
Athens   Auckland   Bangkok   Bogota   Bombay
Buenos Aires   Calcutta   Cape Town   Dar es Salaam
Delhi   Florence   Hong Kong   Istanbul   Karachi
Kuala Lumpur   Madras   Madrid   Melbourne
Mexico City   Nairobi   Paris   Singapore
Taipei   Tokyo   Toronto   Warsaw

and associated companies in
Berlin   Ibadan

Copyright © 1998 by Donald H. Matthews

Published by Oxford University Press, Inc.
198 Madison Avenue, New York, New York 10016

Oxford is a registered trademark of Oxford University Press

All rights reserved. No part of this publication may be reproduced,
stored in a retrieval system, or transmitted, in any form or by any means,
electronic, mechanical, photocopying, recording, or otherwise,
without the prior permission of Oxford University Press.

Library of Congress Cataloging-in-Publication Data
Matthews, Donald Henry, 1952–
    Honoring the ancestors : an African cultural interpretation of
Black religion and literature / Donald H. Matthews.
      p.   cm.
    Originally presented as the author's thesis (doctoral)—University
of Chicago.
    Includes bibliographical references and index.
    ISBN 0-19-509104-3
    1. Black theology.   2. Afro-Americans—Religion.   3. Spirituals
(Songs)—History and criticism.   I. Title.
BT82.7.M38   1997
230'.089'96073—dc21   97-1140

9 8 7 6 5 4 3 2 1

Printed in the United States of America
on acid-free paper

230.089
m438h

265677

To Ada and Faith,
The first and last of the Ancestors

Preface

This study was first stimulated by my experiences as an overzealous assistant minister at the oldest and largest African American United Methodist church in the San Francisco–Oakland Bay area: Taylor Memorial United Methodist Church. When I asked Dr. Hill for more work, he had me lead the Wednesday night Bible class. This class was frequented by the oldest and most formidable members of the church. These were people who knew how to pray and how to work. This group, as well as another group I worked with—the Action Group—with some notable exceptions, was predominantly female. They were immigrants from the Deep South, mainly Texas and Arkansas, who came to northern California to work in the newly desegregated Navy shipyards and government installations during World War II.

It did not take me long to realize that my seminary education offered little help in interpreting their religious and social experiences. I was enthralled by their stories of life in the segregated South and prejudiced North. I frankly never had realized the excruciating price that my elders, men and women, had paid in carving out a place of dignity and humanity.

The women told their stories of having to wear dresses of an extraordinarily modest length in order to deflect the "attentions" of white men. This solution, however, seldom was satisfactory, and girls often found themselves on northern-bound trains and buses to protect their sexual choice and bodily integrity.

The men spoke of resisting the efforts of landowners who "suggested" that their wives should work alongside them in the backbreaking work of sharecropping with poor tools on poorer land. These acts of courage also tended to result in midnight train rides north, often just ahead of a lynch mob.

They all spoke of the northern promised land, but it had offered them discrimination, homelessness, and broken dreams rather than the milk and honey of FDR's federal edict, for America was not yet willing to accept them on equal terms. America would accept their labor for the war effort, but the laborers still couldn't buy a Coke at the ten-cent store in downtown Oakland or live in decent family housing.

I was startled to realize that their political sensibilities were closer to Malcolm X than to Martin King and that they had Christian beliefs not to be found in Tillich's or Barth's systematic theologies. It was this combination of deep feeling, resistance, and African-based religious concepts that I could not find in my black theological texts, either. So I was left with their powerful and profound stories without a method of interpretation that did them justice.

This work is an attempt at developing a method that adequately captures the essence of African American religious experience. It seeks to understand what the black religious community already knows yet is constrained from affirming. It was fortuitous that I found scholars at the University of Chicago and the Graduate Theological Union at Berkeley, California, who were interested in narrative and dialectical ways of knowing. They helped me sort out various theories and finally engage in a hermeneutics of retrieval. Robert MacAfee Brown and Robert Michael Franklin allowed me to explore narrative theology in black and white. James Gustafson's noted yearlong seminar in theological ethics gave me the opportunity to delve into the life of Nate Shaw and to reflect on the relationship of theology to the social sciences.

I rediscovered the earlier works of African American social scientists and those nameless bards of the African American spirituals who, due to their creative genius and religious and political sensitivities, developed a method that was contiguous with their lives. The writings of James Cone and Charles Long were fundamental in guiding me in the direction I needed to go.

In the following pages, I will give flesh to these ideas in the hope that those stories I heard at Taylor Memorial will have found a method worthy of their meaning and that others will develop better ways of telling and interpreting their story.

The concepts discussed in this book pre date the controversy over Afrocentricity. I hope that by showing the importance of African culture in the interpretation of black religion by scholars who predate the Afrocentric movement, I will demonstrate the misguided nature of the present controversy.

Chapter 1 is an introduction to some of the intellectual issues that this work addresses. In this chapter I outline the scholarly terrain concerning several of the key issues that confront the scholar of African American culture. I am concerned with the development of a truly dialectical methodology for the interpretation of black religion and literature. I compare a dialectical perspective with dualistic perspectives, which I believe are less adequate in their ability to capture the essence of black culture. The methodology of earlier scholars like W.E.B. Du Bois, Zora Neale Hurston and Melville Herskovitz are championed as the trailblazers of a dialectical methodology that does justice to the cultural, political, and psychological nature of black narration.

Chapter 2 is a more specific presentation of a dialectical methodology as I examine research concerning the exemplar of African American narration: the spiritual. The spiritual serves as both metaphor and methodology in my interpretation of the cultural space generated by Africans in America. I discuss the cultural, political and ethnocentric dialectic of an African American interpretive framework.

Chapter 3 is my theological analysis of the spirituals from a structuralist and postmodern perspective. Although these may seem to be contradictory terms, I believe that African and African American discourse are best represented by a postmodern structuralist model that understands social reality as a fluid and changing phenomenon, yet formed by social and cultural structures. Black religion and literature reflect this postmodern emphasis on narrative creativity but they are always expressed by specific cultural structures in which we can see the imprint of Africa in form and meaning.

Chapter 4 examines the significance of black literary criticism to the black hermeneutic enterprise. I examine the role of religion in the interpretive works of several black literary critics and once again demonstrates the relative adequacy of a cultural structural methodology that predates the present emphasis on post-strucuralism. I claim that this cultural structural methodology does justice to religious phenomena and the African nature of black religion and literature in ways that escapes contemporary black literary theory's fascination with post-structuralist methodology.

Chapter 5 is the application of a "spiritual" cultural structural interpretation to a classic text of African American narration. I hope that this chapter makes clear the power of this approach for the study of African American religion and literature.

Chapter 6 and the postscript reinforce the relevance of the African cultural interpretive model and the need to understand the African American journey as captured in religion and literature as a part of the larger African diaspora that is still developing throughout our modern world.

Acknowledgments

Archie Smith Jr., Durwood Foster, and Charles and Margie McCoy in Berkeley were instrumental In challenging me to think in traditional and nontraditional ways about black theology. James Gustafson, David Tracy, John Comaroff, Robin Lovin, Don Browning, James Fernandez, and Lauren Berlant at the University of Chicago were my mentors in a project that was as difficult to create as it was to conceive.

I owe a special debt of thanks to these scholars who were not willing to allow me to think conventionally about unconventional subject matter. Gustafson and Tracy demonstrated that they not only were the leading Protestant and Catholic theologians of this era but, more important, also were gentle but persistent advisors who would settle for nothing less than an indigenous interpretation of African American religion. Comaroff, chair of the Anthropology Department at Chicago, insisted that I prove my thesis in such a way that even the best of British-trained anthropologists of African religion could appreciate the relationship between African and African American religion. The Rev. Dr. Jeremiah Wright and Trinity Church served as a living embodiment of the black theological principles I have attempted to delineate.

My homeboys, Don F. Guest and William J. Vance, were there for me through thick and thin. My homegirls, Gwen Barnes, Dorset Perine, Brenda Gregoire, Linda Jenkins, Jan Lowe, Linda Thomas, Joyce Williams, and Cheryl Ann Kirk Duggan, were generous with their support and their spirituality in ways that I still struggle to understand. Phil Blackwell allowed me to put the spirituals in action with my partners in service: Steve Casmier, Matt Johnson, Ted Manley, Angela Harris, Lee Cornelius, and Tukufu.

Martha Hoaglund introduced me to *All God's Dangers* in a Christmas gift that made me realize the presence and power of black religiosity in black narration. Lela Johnson, Melanie Tyler, Joy Browne, Lisa Douglass, Liza Hendricks, Doug Cunningham, and Rebecca Asedillo all helped me keep body and soul together through their friendship and encouragement.

The scholars in the religion departments at Central Michigan and Temple Universities—especially Roger Hatch, Merlyn Mowrey, Robin Hough, John Raines and Lucy Bregman—gave me the space and encouragement to think new thoughts. My former students—Faread Munir, Ina Fandrich, Joan Martin, Valerie Dixon, and Susanna Schmitt—stimulated my research with their own creative projects.

I owe a debt of gratitude to my colleagues in black theology and ethics—Preston Williams, Peter Paris, Cheryl Townsend Gilkes, Riggins Earl Jr., John Cartwright, and Diana Yeager—who, along with their pungent criticisms, allowed my work to be presented at various conferences.

My greatest debts are owed to my family. My brothers, William and Alvin, taught me how to fight and survive. To the men in my family who passed in the way of black men during the writing of this work—my father, William; my uncle Andrew; and my nephew Alvino—your works were not in vain. To the women, Ada, Esther, Amanda, Carole, Mary, Annie, Tracy, and Tanya—your spirits made this work possible. To my loving wife and soul-mate, JoAnna, and children, Jonathan, William, Joanna, Jon, and Faith, the world belongs to you.

I owe a special debt to Cynthia Read, my editor at Oxford, who persevered despite many obstacles and trials. I give special thanks to Roger Hatch who, with his excellent editorial assistance and sensitivity to black religion and culture, helped me turn a dissertation into a readable text. Roger not only gave me my first job at Central Michigan but also helped me write my first book. And they say that angels no longer exist! I also appreciate his wife and co-intellectual, Joyce Baugh, for sharing him during our extended working periods. Joyce not only is an able scholar and chair of the Political Science Department at Central Michigan University but also does a mean electric slide.

This work was completed during a postdoctoral fellowship at Washington University in the African and African American Studies and Religion Programs, chaired by Gerald Early and Patout Burns, respectively. Dr. Early and his assistants, Adele Tuchler and Raye Riggins, provided the hospitality and space that made the revisions possible. I hope that this book meets some of the expectations of those both seen and unseen.

Thanks also to Gene Romanosky for his special assistance in the final stages of the editing process. A special thanks is due to Rev. Betty Williams and Rev. Troy Bonner, who invited me to discuss this material at the Black History celebration at the State University of New York at Buffalo.

Come, taste, and see that the Lord is good!

St. Louis, Missouri   D. H. M.
September 1997

Contents

HONORING *the* ANCESTORS

Interpretation and the African American Situation

The black theology movement is suffering from a crisis of method. This crisis is a reflection of the identity crisis that has plagued African Americans since their status as indentured servants and bondsmen and bondswomen was altered to become that of slaves and chattel. This altering of social relationships and identity, this ignoble differentiation of African persons, was not simply the creation of an Other. It was violation of one of the greatest moral achievements of Western civilization, namely, that one should never treat a subject as an object. This practical violation of the Golden Rule and Kantian ethics has had severe moral and social consequences for Africans and Europeans alike. It has caused both groups to reformulate their identity, and it has led to devastating suffering and loss of life for both Africans and Europeans. The unceasing tribal wars in Africa, the loss of life in the Middle Passage and the plantations, and the eventual heart-rending losses suffered by Americans in the Civil War were only some of the negative consequences of this reconfiguration of African humanity.[1]

In order to accomplish the objectification of the African, Europeans not only had to alter their own hard-earned moral principles but also had to suppress the African roots of their own European moral, religious, and intellectual heritage. The Western human sciences became active leaders in the suppression of Africans and the African-Egyptian roots of Western civilization. This suppression included an obfuscation of the contribution that the black Moors of Spain made to the founding and establishment of the European intellectual community. Shakespeare's ambivalent rendering of Othello is an appropriate metaphor of Europe's acknowledgment of both the poverty and the vitality of Africa and its fear of both.

Any facts or ideas that contradicted Western ethnocentrism had to be suppressed to justify the African slave trade's role in Europe's expansion. This knowledge of the African contribution to Western civilization became dangerous, threatening Western European hegemony and its views of the superiority of Europe's civilization over the denizens of the Dark Continent. Acknowledgment of the humanity of Africans and of the African roots of Western civilization would have undermined any arguments about the chattel status of African Americans.

It is ironic that even a leisurely walk through the British Museum can put to rest any notions of African inferiority. Instead, visitors would be impressed by the genius of African people, and those of us from America should be impressed by the psychic energy that must have been expended in suppressing the African contributions to Western civilization. African people also may feel a sense of loss, as the intricate pieces of West African art in the British Museum of Mankind seem to cry out for the recognition they deserve as magnificent creations of a people whose cultural heritage has long been denied.

While the wealth that Europe gained from the African slave trade allowed for the rapid development of capitalism, it also provided the impetus for a decrease of conscience and consciousness of African humanity and therefore a diminution of the humanity of Europe. A Europe that was awakening from its Dark Ages desperately needed this newfound source of African wealth for its own mercantile and industrial development. Perhaps it also needed a worthy adversary, which it first found among the black Moors who long had threatened its borders and later found among the black masses of an unknown continent.

Although the psychic cost of the suppression of the reality of African humanity was great for the European community, it did provide many economic benefits. Of course, the cost to Africans was far greater, for Africans paid in the disruption of their civilization. Captivity, forced migration, and denigration were but some of the prices paid by Africans. The greatest price, however, would be paid by those of the African diaspora to come, who would pay with the destruction of their way of life and their sense of communal identity.

The travel diaries and reports of early European explorers of West African civilizations are replete with a sense of awe and fear of a world that was the same and yet different from their own. To quote T. S. Eliot: "they had the experience but missed the meaning" of the cultures they encountered.[2]

The pluralistic religious sensibility of West African cultures stood in direct contrast to the monotheism of the Western religions of Judaism, Christianity, and Islam. Yet West Africans also had "divine kings" and a feudal society, as did these early European explorers. Many of these African rulers also were adherents of Islam, a faith that shared the monotheism of European nations but also was a main competitor for the economic goods, territory, and the hearts and minds of modern people.

Europeans' curiosity toward Africans soon turned to loathing as economic factors became more important than moral principles. Africans became a puzzlingly similar, yet different culture, which rapidly would be viewed as inferior to European society, for there was money to be made and a faith to defend. James Baldwin eloquently recounts this state of affairs:

> The Black man's first encounter with the West—by which I mean, mainly, the Christian church—brought him devastation and death. We are only, now, beginning to recover, are beginning, out of the most momentous diaspora in human memory, to rediscover and recognize each other. This is a global matter, and the denouement of this encounter will be bloody and severe: precisely because it demolishes the morality, to say nothing of the definitions, of the Western world.[3]

Those Africans who were transported to North America paid a heavy price for their captivity. The unbending nature of American Protestantism denied slaves the freedom of an exact remembrance and practice of past rites and rituals. Religion and cultural behavior that could be traced to African origins were suppressed. Their languages were silenced, and their captors required them to learn a new tongue.

African communities in the United States would adopt the manners but not necessarily the beliefs of their Anglo-European captors. In so doing, they created a new religion and culture that were the product of complex dialectical forces born of both European and African influences. If the project of Europeans was to tame "savages," then African Americans conformed while maintaining the "savage" edge of their African heritage in structural ways. This savage voice would turn out to be the most eloquent produced on American shores.

In the evangelistic eruption of the Great Awakenings of the mid-eighteenth to mid-nineteenth centuries, Africans in America encountered a religion similar enough in structure and style to their African religions to provide a vehicle for their own beliefs. This relatively quick adaptation by African Americans to a religion that they previously had rejected was proof of the survival of a religious sensibility that had been "invisible" to their captors.[4]

This book is an attempt to get the ball rolling toward a hermeneutic method and an appreciation for the place of the African religious perspective in the theological interpretation of African American religion. There is general recognition that this task is important and enormous. The African American theologian Gayraud Wilmore writes:

> The problem of creating a black hermeneutic is infinitely more difficult. . . . It has to do with the intricate work of unpacking the mythology, folklore, and ethical norms of the black community as reflected in its oral tradition and literature, in order to uncover the ways in which blacks have linguistically and otherwise communicated their provisional and ultimate concerns and solutions in an exploitative and racist society. Something like what Franz Fanon did for the people of Algeria and the French-speaking Caribbean needs to be done for oppressed blacks in the United States. Such a black hermeneutic would deal with the morphology of black English, the meaning of black music, poetry, the novel, the dance and, as Mitchell suggested, not only with the content, but the accent and cadence of black preaching.[5]

This, indeed, is an enormous task, far too much for any one scholar, especially in a single work. I hope to make a dent in this problem, however, by demonstrating how methodologies that do not recognize the dialectical nature of African American religion unwittingly have hindered the development of an adequate African American narrative hermeneutic.

The concepts of structuralism, hermeneutics, and dialectics reflect the life situation of the intellectual community, not the African American religious community. Although I will criticize my African American colleagues who also are forced to write a story that was meant to be spoken, preached, prayed, or sung, I do acknowledge their difficulty in writing about a religious experience in which even the written word is a betrayal of our stolen languages. In writing what follows, I attempt to fashion a common voice with which we can continue this crucial conversation.

Methodological Diversion: Dualistic Interpretations of African American Religion

Political Dualism: Transformation or Accommodation

Benjamin Mays's *The Negro's God as Reflected in His Literature* represents the first theological investigation of African American religion by an African American scholar trained in the academic study of theology and the social sciences.[6] This marks Mays as the intellectual forerunner of the contemporary black theology movement. In addition to Mays's role as a scholar and theologian, Mays has had a tremendous impact on black religious leadership. As president of Morehouse College in Atlanta, he supervised the education of many prominent black pastors and professionals. For example, it was at Morehouse that Martin Luther King Jr. found an intellectual mentor and role model in the person of Mays.

Mays attempted to explain the theological meanings of African American conceptions of God through a study of what he termed "mass" and "classical" black literature. Mays cites the spirituals as examples of a mass Negro literature that reflects a theological view that holds a "compensatory" view of God found in traditional, orthodox Christianity. It is in contrast to "classical" black literature, where ideas of social transformation are more prevalent. By "compensatory," Mays is referring to the position that believers will receive compensation in the next world for the sufferings incurred in this one. Black Christians' adoption of this belief was thought to account for a lack of social activism by many black churches. Rather than actively oppose social evil, these churches emphasized the rewards that would be gained in heaven in return for silent suffering. In contrast to this "compensatory" position, many churches believed that the church was to be a principal agent in bringing the Kingdom of God to earth. Mays's theological education probably was influenced by the Social Gospel movement of the early twentieth century. That movement advocated the church's need to be active in the social transformation of society.

Mays qualifies this stance in the conclusion of his section on the spirituals when he writes that the theme of social protest is dominant in several spirituals, such as "Go Down, Moses" and "Oh Freedom." Mays believes that African Americans saw their own situation as parallel to that of the Hebrews in bondage in Egypt: "It seems that the Negro was accustomed to interpret Negro slavery in terms of Egyptian bondage. Throughout such interpretations, he implied that as freedom came to the Hebrews it would come to the Negro. The approach is subtle."[7] This subtle approach of the spirituals constitutes a method of discourse that lies at the very heart of African American religious expression in the context of the dialectic of racist oppression.[8]

Other black religious scholars later would disagree with Mays, agreeing instead with Miles Mark Fisher in *Negro Slave Songs in the United States,* who saw the spirituals as being almost exclusively concerned with freedom themes that refer obliquely to Africa as the object of freedom.[9]

My major point here is that Mays's work suffers from a dualistic, nondialectical interpretation of African American religion. Mays's work separates the traditional from the transformational and separates the mass from the class. It represents a forced dichotomy of the African American religious process solely along obvious political lines. As I will suggest, African American religion, when viewed from cultural, political, and ethnocentric dialectical perspectives, reveals a much more nuanced view of the interaction between religion and politics.

Future black theologians and social scientists would follow Mays's political dualism and seek to determine the relationship of black religion to the political and social order without an equally strong consideration of its cultural status. I contend that African American religion represents a political statement because it continues or transforms African religious concerns in its culturally specific narrative style.

These cultural statements are seen in the everyday religious lives of people whose religion is a way to resist political and cultural subjugation. These cultural statements also provide coherence to their world and help them oppose the prevailing cultural style. Culture can be viewed as a prime way in which people, especially oppressed people, encode their religious and political desires. Culture is a prism that dialectically reveals, hides, and disguises social practices.[10]

Instead of focusing solely on such overt themes as liberation or accommodation, black theologians also may have been able to develop a more nuanced view of black religion as a repository for African and African American cultural memories. These memories can serve as an ideological form of resistance to oppression. They exist as a testimony to a religious heritage that could not be destroyed by the brutality of slavery and discrimination.

In this perspective, supposedly innocuous religious forms provide alternative worldviews and can lead to more direct and sustained efforts at revolution and social change. This certainly was the case in the civil rights and black power movements of the twentieth century. However, Mays's methodology, in which stated themes are the primary objects of analysis and interpretation, provides a static view of African American thought along obvious class and political lines. Instead, African American religion should be viewed as a changing, dynamic phenomenon than can adapt itself to prevailing social situations or can transform itself.

Following Mays's lead, African American religion came to be seen as a static entity that either promoted or inhibited social change. Its African character—of which improvisation and spontaneity, call and response, polyrhythms, and intense feeling are main features—was ignored in the attempt to delineate particular progressive or socially accommodative themes. In other words, the method of interpretation did not fit the method of the people under study.

This acultural view of Mays can also be seen in the work of Joseph Washington. Washington fails to recognize what I term the the cultural dialectical character of the spirituals as the carrier of African meanings. Although Washington recognizes that the spirituals were the result of the African and slave experiences, he asserts that blacks have left this cultural form behind them in slavery:

> The spirituals originated in the souls of slaves, created out of Christianity provided by whites and the American experience. Spirituals were left behind by blacks with the slave experience.
> . . . The evidence is all in! It is clear from the history books and present observations that blacks have carried over into the American experience African practices but not African beliefs.[11]

These passages demonstrate the ethnocentric dialectical denial of the African cultural past that followed in the wake of Mays's work. Washington argues that African American religion may have retained the form but not the meaning of African religion. This dualistic position not only creates a political dualism but also contributes to a cultural dualism because the African religious foundations of African American religion are obscured. This opposition of form and function continues to plague black theologians. I will examine this methodological dualism at some length in this chapter, using the work of African American historian and theologian Albert Raboteau as an example of the kind of methodology that is prevalent in the works of major black religious scholars.

This dualistic perspective separates form from function, structure from meaning, and style from content. It is dialectical in understanding African American religion as the result of interaction between the oppressed and the oppressor, but there is little acknowledgment that form also signifies function, that cultural structures continue to carry meaning, and that style often contains content.

Black theologians generally have accepted the premises and problems of this dualistic dialectical methodology and ask either-or questions that require clear, unambiguous responses. A dialectical position, however, calls for a both-and position that acknowledges the presence of both African and American meanings.

African American religion has been concerned with orthodoxy and maintenance, as is any expression of religion, and it also has been concerned with issues of social transformation. African American religion shares African and evangelical Christian American characteristics because it was created out of a social situation that contained both elements. The advantage of the cultural-structural methodology is that it reveals both the political and the cultural structures of African American religion. It does not deny either the political or the religious nature of the religion of African Americans because it is faithful to describing it in its fullness.

By adopting a dualistic, either-or perspective, black theologians have not been able to appreciate the depth of the dialectical nature of African American religion. The adoption of an ethnocentric theological position has contributed to this methodological failure because it does not acknowledge the presence of African cultural characteristics.[12]

As we shall see, because black theologians adopted the methodological position of Mays rather than that of DuBois, they have argued within the closed, nondialectical discourse of traditional Christian theology, which finds meaning primarily in written Christian doctrines and themes. These doctrines generally are found in doctrinal statements, a mode of discourse which itself reflects a Western bias that favors literate over narrative means of expression.

This method of analysis has led black theologians to overlook the narrative-based meanings of African American Christians. Black Christians seldom were allowed the privilege of putting their innermost thoughts and beliefs on paper. During slavery, most blacks were not allowed to write, and even the slave narratives were meant to convince their American and European audiences that they shared the same ideologies and therefore the same humanity as their readers. This dualistic methodological bias has led to the development of black theologies that examine ideal Christian representations more than actual black practice.

Black theologians should no longer feel obligated to ignore the contribution of African concepts in African American religion simply to gain European American acceptance. This methodological dualism by black theologians ultimately contributes to racist premises that denigrate all things black or African.

Contemporary African American Historiography

Cultural Dualism: Structure or Meaning

Raboteau's work is a continuation of this cultural dualistic perspective, yet it also is an excellent example of a thorough use of narrative sources of slave religion by an African American religious historian and theologian. Raboteau successfully demonstrates the complexity of the genesis of African American religion by using slave narratives and other available demographic and literary data. Nevertheless, his interpretive method prevents him from acknowledging the full extent of the African cultural heritage in African American religion. Since I argue that African American spirituals represent the foundation of African American religion, I will center my discussion of Raboteau's method of interpretation around his treatment of African American spirituals. Raboteau is well aware of the debate over the influence of African culture on African American religion. He strives to avoid the argument, but he invariably agrees with those who argue against a significant African influence in African American religion. I believe that his evidence, however, actually contradicts his conclusions and that his method, which stresses overt themes over structurally embedded meanings, prevents him from integrating an African cultural-structural perspective into his work.[13]

Raboteau employs a thoroughly narrative method. He makes ample use of African American slave narratives in various forms: testimonies, sermons, and songs. Raboteau also attends to the structural features of African American religion and the dialectical process which created it, and he conducts a thorough analysis of African American spirituals. In his analysis, he identifies certain features of the spirituals identified by other cultural-structuralist-informed scholars. Raboteau identifies the African heritage that led to the use of call and response, polyrhythms, syncopation, ornamentation, slides, repetition, and forms of bodily movement.[14]

Raboteau, however, contrasts structure with meaning and accordingly asserts that, even though African Americans in the United States may well have retained structural features of African religion, the content is thoroughly Christian:

> Despite the African style of singing, the spirituals, like the "running spirituals" or ring shout, were performed in praise of the Christian God. The names and words of the African gods were replaced by Biblical figures and Christian imagery. African style and European hymnody met and became in the spiritual a new, Afro-American song to express the joys and sorrows of the religion which the slaves had made their own.[15]

Here Raboteau makes the fatal separation between form and meaning. Raboteau's lack of clarity about the theological relevance of African beliefs for African American religion would have been overcome had he recognized how structures carry meanings and had he applied this to his analysis of African American religion. Sometimes he seems to be aware of this, but at other times he offers dualistic interpretations.

The theological significance of Raboteau's statements about the spirituals not only concern the interaction of slavery and oppression but also powerfully indicate the transmission of an African religious heritage that placed a paramount concern on the welfare of the community and extended family. At one level, Raboteau seems to recognize this. In his discussion of the role of freedom in the spirituals, for example, he states:

> Categorizing sacred and secular elements is of limited usefulness in discussing the spirituals because the slave, *following African and biblical tradition* [my emphasis], believed that the supernatural continually impinged on the natural, that divine action constantly took place within the lives

of men, in the past, present and future. It was precisely at the worship and praise services in which the spirituals were so important that the contact between God and man became real for the slaves.[16]

Even though Raboteau's evidence reveals both African and Christian cultural influences in African American religion, his methodological dualism, which separates structures from meaning, guides him to deny the African cultural influence at the level of meaning.

This tendency toward a dualistic interpretation also is found in his discussion of spirit possession, in which he also treats structure and meaning as separate, unrelated phenomena. He makes use of a distinction made by Erika Bourguignon: "What is generally spoken of as 'spirit possession' actually involves two distinct aspects, two distinct levels of ethnographic fact: an observable behavior pattern and a system of cultural beliefs and interpretations. These, however, in turn structure expectations and therefore behavior."[17] Raboteau adds:

> In other words, though not separated in fact, there are two aspects which should be distinguished for the sake of clarity in discussion: the faith context in which the possession experience occurs and the patterned style of outward response by which the ecstatic experience is manifest. On the level of theological interpretation and meaning, African spirit possession differs significantly from the shouting experience found in the revivalist tradition of American evangelicalism.[18]

Raboteau states that the experience of spirit possession in African and African American religion is different on the basis of their differing linguistic referents. This statement leaves readers to wonder how Raboteau is able to verify which deity is possessing the believer. Raboteau does not present evidence that would decide this matter. In fact, how he could know whether an African spirit or the Holy Spirit is at work in the life of the possessed person is not explained.

Raboteau's method and interpretive conclusions reflect a theological approach that itself reflects a narrow form of Christian apologetic that desires to distinguish Christian from "pagan" religious experience. This dualistic argument, which sets African religion against Christian religion, was the prevailing ideology among evangelical Christians. It has been attacked by African theologians and by anthropologists of African and African American religion as a view that severely limits the points of contact between the two cultural worlds.[19]

Other scholars have suggested that a structural approach to spirit possession yields more similarities than differences in these cultural experiences. Sheila Walker, an African American anthropologist specializing in African religions in Africa and in the New World, suggests that possession experiences depend on certain social circumstances and have little to do with theological preferences.[20]

A convincing, though negative, proof that African Americans developed an African style of religion comes from white Americans, who termed African American religious practice "barbaric" because it was overly demonstrative.[21] Even if we granted Raboteau his distinction between structure and meaning, other historians of African American religion also would take issue with the conclusion that black religion was thoroughly Christian to the exclusion of African religious meanings.

Hurston's discussion of the spirituals and possession is instructive. As we shall see, her cultural-structural methodology enabled her to understand that in African religion, as in other forms of behavior, structure or style also is filled with meaning. Hurston recognized in the cultural forms of African Americans the presence of an African heritage that was not acknowledged because of political and social pressures. Black theologians' tendency to advocate a position in which structure or form is separated from meaning is a continuation of an ideology that denies the legitimacy of non-Western cultural forms.

Note on Form and Meaning

A dialectical analysis refuses to separate form from meaning. This means that an acknowledgment of the African form of African American religion is pregnant with the meanings that this form of spirituality evokes and evinces. This semiological understanding of the relation of form to meaning is discussed by the French scholar Roland Barthes in the appropriately titled *Mythologies*:

> What must always be remembered is that myth is a double system; there occurs in it a sort of ubiquity; its point of departure is constituted by the arrival of a meaning. . . . [T]he signification of the myth is constituted by a sort of constantly moving turnstile which presents alternately the meaning of the signifier and its form, a language-object and a metalanguage, a purely signifying and a purely imagining consciousness. This alternation is, so to speak, gathered up in the concept, which uses it like an ambiguous signi-

fier, at once intellective and imaginary, arbitrary and natural. . . . The meaning is always there to present the form; the form is always there to outdistance the meaning. And there never is any contradiction, conflict, or split between the meaning and the form: they are never at the same place. . . . The same thing occurs in the mythical signifier: its form is empty but present, its meaning absent but full. To wonder at this contradiction I must voluntarily interrupt this turnstile of form and meaning, I must focus on each separately, and apply to myth a static method of deciphering, in short, I must go against its own dynamics: to sum up, I must pass from the state of reader to that of mythologist.[22]

Barthes's discussion of the relationship between form and meaning is similar to the popular discussion concerning the relationship between waves and particles in quantum mechanics. Stephen Hawking discusses how the scientific community recognized that light acted as both waves and particles, that waves may sometime behave as particles, and that particles may sometime behave as waves. This duality demonstrates how thoroughly analysts are influenced by the instruments (methods) that they employ to study phenomena. Reality must not be confused with the methods of observation.[23]

The dialectical nature of spiritual theology means two things: (1) The preponderance of African cultural forms in African American religion means that African religious meanings are also present, and (2) there is a free-flowing relationship between the form and themes that are generated by African American religion. Whether feeling is called a structure or a theme, for instance, depends on how the term is defined because in reality feeling operates as both a structure and a theme, as both form and meaning. One can observe the presence of emotion through the bodily movements and the intensity of the performance (form) of the spirituals, and one also can observe the presence of feeling through the use of particular lyrics that emphasize emotional attachments: wishes for freedom, reunification with family members, and so on (meaning). Feeling is intricately related in form and meaning, and it expresses African and African American spirituality.

Cultural-Structural Methodology: Structure and Meaning

Black theologians' tendency to separate structure from meaning is not the norm in African American religious historiography. When Eugene

Genovese discusses the role of religion in the slave community in *Roll, Jordan, Roll: The World the Slaves Made,* he finds convincing evidence of African structures with an African theological or religious orientation.[24] This orientation includes the presence of such African religious ideas as "superstition," a notion of sin, and the sense of debt to ancestors. According to Genovese, these features indicate a distinctively African orientation toward religious ideology in the religious life of African captives in America:

> White contemporaries, resident and nonresident, agreed that the religious life of the slaves embraced much more than religion, anything they were capable of recognizing as Christianity. Most also agreed that the slaves' *religious feeling* [my emphasis], whatever its elements, ran deep. During the war Thomas Wentworth Higginson recounted with wonder and admiration the spirit of the black troops, most of whom had only recently been slaves. Not since Cromwell's time, he exulted, have we seen so religious an army. The blacks called it a "Gospel Army." Among the more significant features of his account are these: the blacks spoke and sang incessantly of Moses and associated him with all the great events of history, including the most recent; their services displayed drumming, clapping, and bodily movement in the African manner; and the praisehouses they built reminded him of nothing so much as a "regular African hut." He observed wisely that the deep religious faith of the slaves had saved them from the dehumanization the abolitionists had feared inevitable under slavery.[25]

Other scholars also recognized the Africanness of the African American worship style, which emphasized rhythms and feeling. Unlike Raboteau, Genovese does not attempt to separate structure from meaning. Genovese recognizes that structure and meaning invariably are related as African Americans created a religion that was a synthesis of African and evangelical Christian elements.

Genovese also discusses African American spirituals more directly in the formation of African American religion:

> The slaves' talent for improvisation, as well as their deep religious conviction, drew expressions of wonder and admiration from almost everyone who heard them sing. The boatmen of Georgia and South Carolina and of the Mississippi River received the most attention and drew the most comment, but the common field hands of the Cotton Belt did not lag far behind in performance. The words "wild" and "weird" recurred

among white observers, from the abolitionists to the slave-holders to the merely curious. . . . Eliza Frances Andrews, listening to the slaves on her plantation singing at a praise-meeting, called their singing "mostly a sort of weird chant that makes me feel all out of myself when I hear it way in the night, too far off to catch the words."[26]

These passages once again emphasize the intense feeling and improvisation found in the spirituals, which also characterize the slaves' West African religious heritage. Although the spirituals were created in a situation of oppression and suffering in America, the cultural tools used to guide religious expressions were African cultural features. The African American community took African structures of meaning, most notably intense structures of feeling, and used them in conjunction with an African-based rhythmic accompaniment to express their deepest theological meanings. The fortuitous development of American evangelism, with its emphasis on emotion and conversion through a form of spirit possession, was made to order for Africans who were seeking a religion of their own.

In addition to his attention to structure, Genovese attempts to show that African American religion also included religious ideas that were decidedly African. He asserts that black religion was similar to African religion in several ways: the slaves' lack of an idea of original sin, their beliefs about spiritual visitation, and other "magical" beliefs, all of which would run counter to the evangelical Christian notions of the day.[27]

These beliefs reflected West African religious views more than those of evangelical Protestant Christianity. European and American theology long have had difficulty incorporating folk religious beliefs and experiences into their theological categories because they have always seen theology as part and parcel of a Western Christianity and civilization that distinguished itself from these very folk expressions of belief.[28]

Genovese notes that the slaves, in distinction from the prevailing Euro-American community, developed an idea of being "debtors to the ages." This ideology fostered a sense of responsibility to those who came before, an ideology reminiscent of reverence for the ancestors in African traditional religion. Once again, Genovese sees this view as different from the prevailing American religious ethos in which Americans saw themselves as the heirs, not the debtors, of history.[29]

Another historian of African American religion and culture, Lawrence Levine, contributed to this discussion of the genesis and cultural character of African American religion. In his assessment of the ethics and theology of the slave community, Levine examines the central place of the spirituals:

> The spirituals are testament not only to the perpetuation of significant elements of an older world view among the slaves but also to the continuation of a strong sense of community. Just as the process by which the spirituals were created allowed for simultaneous individual and communal creativity, so their very *structure* [my emphasis] provided simultaneous outlets for individual and communal expression. The overriding antiphonal structure of the spirituals—the call-and-response pattern which Negroes brought with them from Africa and which was reinforced in America by the practice of lining out hymns—placed the individual in continual dialogue with his community. . . . Here again slave music confronts us with evidence which indicates that, however seriously the slave system may have diminished the central commonality that had bound African societies together, it was never able to destroy it totally or to leave the individual atomized and psychically defenseless before his white masters. In fact, the form and structure of slave music presented the slave with a potential outlet for his individual feelings even while it continually drew him back into the communal presence and permitted him the comfort of basking in the warmth of the shared assumptions of those around him.[30]

Levine demonstrates an awareness of the role of African cultural structures of meaning in the development of African American religion. Yet this awareness of the culturally dialectical nature of African American religion does not prevent Levine from also recognizing themes that are concerned with African American freedom in the New World.

Levine's emphasis on the structure of the spirituals is important. Examining the structure of the spirituals, Levine sees that the slaves created a mode of approaching their oppressive reality that is reminiscent of the African past. The call-and-response structure of the spirituals allowed for communal creativity, solidarity, and interaction, which strengthened the slaves in their struggle for survival. This African mode of action helped the slaves maintain a sense of community and care which reflected their African communities.

Levine also notes the personal nature of early African American theology found in the spirituals: "The God the slaves sang of was neither remote nor abstract, but as intimate, personal, and immediate as the gods of Africa had been. 'O when I talk I talk wid God,' 'Massa Jesus is my bosom friend,' 'I'm goin' to walk with [talk with, live with, see] King Jesus by myself, by myself,' were refrains that echoed through the spirituals."[31] Levine summarizes his analysis of the spirituals in this way:

> The religious music of the slaves is almost devoid of feelings of depravity or unworthiness, but is rather, as I have tried to show, pervaded by a sense of change, transcendence, ultimate justice, and personal worth. The spirituals have been referred to as "sorrow songs," and in some respects they were. The slaves sang of "rollin' thro' an unfriendly world," of being "a-trouble in de mind," . . . of feeling like a "motherless child," "a po' little orphan chile in de worl'," a "home-e-less child," of fearing that "Trouble will bury me down."[32]

The presence of metaphors that emphasized freedom and justice was also recognized by Mays and Fisher. Here we see the development of a distinctive African American feature of American religion. This emphasis on earthly freedom cannot be traced directly to American evangelical religion, which, instead, emphasized spiritual salvation. Fisher has interpreted the desire for freedom as a desire for a return to freedom to the African situation or as a desire for freedom in their new home. Regardless, this freedom motif consistently appears in African American religion, along with an African-based cultural ideology that helped to preserve their communal and personal identity.[33]

In many ways, Levine's cultural-structural assessment of the spirituals is similar to that of Raboteau and Genovese, who note that the spirituals are marked by the African style of improvisation, call and response, and polyrhythms. Levine and Genovese—but not Raboteau—also see the presence of African beliefs and practices in the meanings and structures of African American religion.

Levine also shares Genovese's assessment of the distinctiveness of African American theology's conception of sin, a view decidedly different than the Christian idea of original sin. This observation also contrasts with Raboteau's assessment that the theology of African Americans was thoroughly Christian.

These insights also are found in the voluminous and thorough study of African American spirituals by John Lovell. Lovell also finds African influences in the creation of the spirituals, the spirituals' sense of social and personal transformation, the concern for family and community, and a concern for the natural order.[34]

Lovell agrees with Levine that the spirituals' structure and performance are signifiers of an African American religious orientation that emphasizes the personal relationship of the creation to the Creator. The spirituals also encouraged and reflected a religious orientation that encourages individual expression within the context of community needs and actions, yet the presence of improvisation always left the possibility for individuality and novelty. That great African American mystic, preacher, and theologian Howard Thurman also found the spirituals to be particularly reflective of African American religion.[35]

The personal style of African American spirituals is one of the persistent features of African American religion. This personalism, in which personal relationships are maintained with the divine community, is part of the African cultural heritage. This African heritage of personal relationships with the divine made it easier for slaves to accept the evangelical religion of the Great Awakenings. The revivalist movements in the United States placed an emphasis on personal faith similar to African religious ideology. When this personal view of religion was combined with the African sensitivity to the expression of feeling in community, the slave community began the process of developing their unique religious perspective, a perspective best found in African American spirituals.

This personalism in slave religion also may help to explain the receptivity of the black ministerial community to the Boston personalism of the 1930s and 1940s, a philosophy that became one of foundations for Martin Luther King's theological perspective. Scholars who have interpreted the life and work of King have overlooked the origins of personalism in the black community as a survival of an African perspective.[36]

The preceding discussion of methodology was meant to accomplish two purposes. The first objective was to demonstrate the interpretive importance of a cultural-structural dialectical approach in interpreting African American religion. Scholars who employ this kind of methodology invariably are impressed with the African nature of African American religion, and they use these insights to give a broader and more culturally complex interpretation of African American religion. By contrast, theologians who interpret African American religion from a dualist perspective invariably deny the presence of African-based meanings in African American religion. These theologians separate structure and meaning, resulting in a denial of the African influence on African American religion.

The second purpose was to identify the cultural structures—both stylistic and substantive features—that characterize African American religion by examining previous research on African American spirituals. This research revealed a consensus about the main structural features of the spirituals: rhythmic structures that were improvisational, antiphonal, and polyrhythmic; intense emotional states; themes of family and freedom; and an intimacy toward the human, divine, and natural communities.

These features can be used as hermeneutic guides for interpreting African American narratives and texts. Using these features gives the advantage of using an interpretive framework that reflects African American religion and culture and avoids relying on categories derived from Western theological perspectives. This does not mean that African or African American religion is totally distinct from Western theological meanings, for, in large part due to the Great Awakenings, American Christianity shares many of the religious practices found in African and African American religion.

I am arguing that African American religion should be judged against its own set of standards and not against those of a Western, rationalistic, literary theology.

African and Spirituals' Narrative Style

Insights by scholars about the importance of African religious style point to an important methodological procedure for interpreting African American personal and social narratives. If attention is paid to African ritual meanings and drama in examining the narratives of African Americans, these narratives reveal the presence of a cultural pattern that has its counterpart in traditional African religion.

This pattern, which I refer to as a spiritual's theological style, has the same ritual structure that characterizes the ritual performance of West African mythic tragedy. This African mythic dramaturgic style has been explicated most clearly in the dramatic writings and literary criticism of Wole Soyinka. Soyinka was the first African writer awarded the Nobel Prize for literature, and his work has played a large role in popularizing the study of West African culture. One of his plays, *Death and the King's Horseman,* is noted for its reenactment of Yoruban narrative myths from West Africa.

Soyinka and critics of his work note that it is based on the dialectic of creation-destruction or disintegration-rejuvenation-reintegration that has been described so thoroughly in the works of cultural anthropologists. A realization that this ritual pattern also is a feature of African American spirituals shifts the interpretive framework for scholars of African American religion.

For instance, Mays stated that he thought of the spirituals as encompassing otherworldly themes, which were supposed to reflect an evangelical "orthodox" Christianity, which, in turn, was a rejection of themes of social transformation. However, if one examines African American spirituals in light of the West African notions of tragedy, one is struck by the remarkable similarity of structural styles.

The style of the spirituals, which was supposed to reflect African Americans' dependence on an otherworldly Christian evangelism, may predate Christian evangelicalism through its relationship to this West African mythic style, a structural style that in its Yoruban context reflects a religious philosophy in which creation and destruction, much like that of the Christian passion narration, are parts of a ritual drama first played out by divine actors.[37]

In the Yoruban context, the worshipers of particular deities reenact a mythic narrative in which the god and the human community are the victims of destructive actions, which then are followed by and therefore superseded by acts of creation and community. The theological significance is that even in the acts of greatest destruction there is potential for rejuvenation and the reintegration of community.

One well-known myth concerns the origin of the founder of the Yoruban people, the divinity Shango. Shango once was a king who because of his drunkenness caused the destruction of many of his people. The remorseful Shango kills himself, but upon his death he is elevated to the status of deity as the god of thunder and lightning. This structural style is similar to the process in the African American spirituals; that is, the people are victims of destructive acts, but there always is the possibility of a divine intervention that will reverse the misfortunes of the people. Similar to the Yoruban context, there is hope in the possibility of divine intervention.

In the African American church, I often have heard the phrase "We didn't cry the blues, we sang the blues." This means that African Americans were able to produce expressions of community out of their sorrow and oppression. Another such aphorism is the often-heard sermon on the Israelites' refusal to sing their songs in the strange land of their captivity. This passage is based on the account of the Babylonian captivity found in the book of Psalms 137:1–4 [RSV]:

> By the waters of Babylon, there we sat down and wept, when we
>   remembered Zion.
> On the willows there
>   we hung up our lyres.
> For there our captors
>   required of us songs,
> and our tormentors mirth, saying,
> "Sing us one of the songs of Zion!"
> How shall we sing the LORD's song in a foreign land?

The sermon that follows is a commentary on the remarkable fact that African Americans have been able to sing their songs of the Lord, the spirituals, in the land of their captivity. Once again, the ability to produce expressions of community in the situation of oppression is stressed as a unique feature of African American religion, just as it is in the Yoruban context.

Therefore, it was not necessary for African Americans to be dependent on "traditional" Christianity to develop this tragic sense of hope even within tragedy. Once again we see the effect of an African religious survival in the African American community in the New World.

In other words, the scholar need not "blame" this feature of African American religion on the black community's adoption of a traditional orthodox Christian position. This religious orientation may have developed from both African and Christian influences. It could be that this underlying African philosophy found a ready partner in an evangelical religious revivalism that stressed the possibility of salvation and spiritual renewal.

Religious conversion in the African American community, as we will see in the case study of Nate Shaw in chapter 6, follows this same pattern of disintegration-rejuvenation-reintegration. Shaw's conversion allowed him, and African American slaves before him, to be reborn into the African American mythic and community ethos that understood life to be a process of creation out of destruction.

265677

ALBRIGHT COLLEGE LIBRARY

Cultural Contact and Cultural Space

The Dialectics of Negation and Resistance

The Spirituals: "A Space to Fit One's Heart Into"

Dialectic I: The Cultural Dialectic

Evangelical Christianity: Negation of African Cultural Traditions   The contact between Europeans and Africans in the New World led to a new arrangement of cultural space (see figure 1). The plantation economy developed an arrangement of cultural space to define the limits of Africans' spirit. The success of the political economy of the slave system necessitated the negation of traditional African culture in order to destroy any hopes of social cohesion among blacks that would lead to revolts. The countryside was where the maroons in Jamaica and escaped slaves in Haiti were able to organize outside the restricted cultural space of slavery in order to mount revolts and social protests. In the United States, blacks sought the cultural space of the North to organize with other abolitionists in the quest to end slavery. Thus on the slave plantations, the cultural space left to Africans would be contested in the secret places of the minds and hearts of slaves in the secret spaces of the plantations.

The most remarkable fact about the development of the African

American spirituals is that they were developed in the secret cultural space of the African captives. In general, whites did not know the Negro spirituals existed until the Civil War, when black soldiers sang their spirituals around the camp fires at night. It is amazing that this powerful musical genre was developed out of sight in a system in which surveillance of slaves was thought to be the key to their domination.

How would Foucault have explained the possibility of the development of the spirituals in secret, just when methods of modern surveillance were being put in place? Not only did slaveowners and their hired overseers keep close watch over their African captives but also they relied on informants within the slave community itself. Nevertheless, Africans developed their spirituals in the image of their African heritage.

Charles Long, the dean of African American religious scholarship, has captured the importance of this African heritage in the religion of blacks in America:

> If not the content of culture, a characteristic mode of orienting and perceiving reality has probably persisted. We know, for example, that a great majority of slaves came from West Africa, and we also know from the studies of Daryll Forde that West Africa is a cultural as well as a geographical unit. Underlying the empirical diversity of languages, religions and social forms, there is, according to Forde, a structural unity discernible in language and religious forms. With the breakdown of the empirical forms of language and religion as determinants for the social group, this persisting structural mode and the common situation as slaves in America may be the basis for the persistence of an African style among the descendants of the Africans. . . .
>
> So even if they had no conscious memory of Africa, the image of Africa played an enormous part in the religion of the blacks. The image of Africa, an image related to historical beginnings, has been one of the primordial religious images of great significance. It constitutes the religious revalorization of the land, a place where the natural and ordinary gestures of the blacks were and could be authenticated. In this connection one can trace almost every nationalistic movement among the blacks and find Africa to be the dominating and guiding image.[1]

Suppression of African religious rituals led to a suppression of African traditional religiosity. Nevertheless, African culture survived in a structural manner, in which African style became the container for African American religious practice. The emphasis on faith as a deeply felt emotional experience of the divine, along with its African stylistic features,

Figure 1
The Spiritual Narrative Dialectic

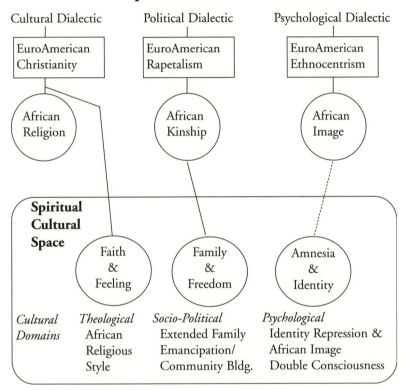

Cultural Dialectic

EuroAmerican
Christianity

African
Religion

Political Dialectic

EuroAmerican
Rapetalism

African
Kinship

Psychological Dialectic

EuroAmerican
Ethnocentrism

African
Image

Spiritual Cultural Space

Faith
&
Feeling

Family
&
Freedom

Amnesia
&
Identity

Cultural Domains

Theological
African
Religious
Style

Socio-Political
Extended Family
Emancipation/
Community Bldg.

Psychological
Identity Repression &
African Image
Double Consciousness

revealed this presence of spirit. Spontaneity, improvisation, call and response, polyrythms, and bodily movements became the way African religion was expressed.

Much of modern psychological theory is based on the idea that modern people are cut off from their feelings. African Americans, however, have developed a religious perspective that continually keeps them in touch with their deepest hopes and fears. This religion of faith and feeling allows blacks to express their sorrows and their joys.

In black religious expression, men are allowed to display their emotions without fear of being thought effeminate or somehow less manly. This space is spiritual space because it involves the worshipers in encountering the divine world in a way that allows them to get in touch with their own guilt and anxiety. During pastoral prayers, which always are accompanied by music, worshipers often are able to restore psychic wholeness through direct experience with the divine. The rhythms of music provide a way for worshipers to enter into a liminal space between heaven and earth and then to emerge as whole members of the community.

Thee Smith has written helpfully about the role of the spirituals in the development of African American religion. Smith's idea that blacks conjured their religion is a useful way to understand the process of cultural creativity in the black slave quarters. Smith concludes that performing the spirituals evoked an intersubjective mood by which the worshipers were able to apprehend the divine.[2] However, I agree instead with Jahn Jahnheinz, who argued that in the spirituals Africans in America were invoking God in a fashion that was similar to traditional African religious practice.[3]

Traditional black church phrases such as "the Spirit paid us a visit today" or "call on the Spirit!" point to the spirituals as an invocation of God's presence and not as something that induces a psychological mood that readies the person to view the presence of the divine.

Slave narratives and spiritual autobiographies also emphasize the evocative nature of religion for African Americans. The mourning bench, where worshipers sought the presence of God's spirit, and the evangelical Great Awakenings of the eighteenth and nineteenth centuries bear witness to this evocative process of spiritual possession.[4] The Negro spiritual "Kum ba Yah" or "Come by Here" is another testimony to the way in which African captives invoked the presence of the Spirit. It is a simple, direct song in which worshipers ask the spirit of God to attend to their cries for the divine presence:

Come by here, my Lord, come by here.
Come by here, my Lord, come by here.
Come by here, my Lord, come by here.
Oh, Lord, come by here.
Someone's crying, Lord, come by here. (*repeat two times*)
Oh, Lord, come by here.
Someone needs you, Lord, come by here. (*repeat two times*)
Oh, Lord, come by here.

The creation of the spirituals was, indeed, an act of conjuration. It was and remains a truly spiritual or religious act, not to be confused with a psychological act or disposition. When African captives called for the presence of the divine, the spirit(s) paid a visit to the worshiping community.

Smith's emphasis on blacks' use of the Bible (a logocentric process in which the written word of God, the Bible, takes precedence) and his use of a methodology that privileges a nonreligious, figurative reading of African American religion, actually hide the true power of the spirituals in African American religious life, namely, that the spirituals were used by Africans to create a religious world of their own. The creation of the spirituals and the performance of the spirituals created a spiritual-cultural space in spite of and in resistance to the dominant society's effort to negate the cultural world of Africans in America. Although this has psychological as well as social implications, it never can simply be reduced to them.

Despite Africans' subordinate status, African culture has had a great effect on the dominant American culture. Various historians have attempted to delineate the effects of African religious sensibilities on the development of evangelical religion. It is obvious that black sacred music has had a tremendous effect on the worship life of American churches. Most Protestant hymnals have at least a token representation of Negro spirituals as part of their permanent liturgical repertoire. In a truly dialectical situation, both parties are influenced by the other. Although Africans may have had much of the content of their religion suppressed by a more powerful social group, nevertheless, they have been able to influence the culture of a developing project called the United States of America.

Dialectic II: The Political Dialectic

Social Oppression and Communal Structure: Negation of Social Cohesion
Family is the central mode of organization in African life. It is a political, social, and religious entity. In Africa, family was a religious as well as a political and social institution. The rapetalistic oppression* of slavery and racism sought to cripple and destroy African family life. The spirituals, with their emphasis on family themes, reveal the their resistance to this oppressive system. Heaven is the place where family members will reunite despite being forcefully separated here on earth. Heaven is more than a meeting with God, it is the biggest family reunion of all time.[5]

> I want to see my mother,
> I want to see my mother,
> I want to see my mother,
> Going to live with God.
> I want to see my brother, (*repeat*)
> Going to live with God.
> I want to see my sister, (*repeat*)
> Going to live with God.
> I want to see my father, (*repeat*)
> Going to live with God.

DuBois and John Lovell mention the prominent place the mother played in the spirituals. The deepest desire of captive Africans was to be reunited in heaven with their mothers. DuBois mentions how the absence of fatherly references also speaks volumes about the familial status of the slaves. Where the father often was forced into being absent or where the mother was forced to mate with various males in order to produce children, it is understandable that fatherhood would be an ambiguous role in the slave family's life. Mother, however, was the center of everyone's familial consciousness and provided the fulcrum that balanced family life.[6]

---

*My term for the confluence of sexual, economic, and racial oppression.

The power of the modern world is its ability to impose symbols and values on its populace: "the dialectics of the bourgeois culture . . . has produced a general industrial culture the essential characteristic of which is the continuous production and consumption of cultural symbols, values, norms, and life styles at all levels of sophistication and educational differentiations."[7]

Creating and performing spirituals were acts of resistance to the negation of African culture in the New World. They gave value to what had become valueless: the African family. They gave voice to what could not be uttered: the desire for freedom. They gave expression to life-affirming values in a style that reflected African structures of feeling. The spirituals created a cultural space wherein Africans could put their hearts without fear of them being ripped apart. Creating this cultural space was a dialectical process in which Africans affirmed in their sacred music precisely what was being negated in their everyday world.

This space created by the spirituals bears directly on issues of African American psychology. Psychologists and therapists have noted African Americans' reluctance to accept the tenets of modern psychology, with its denial of the spiritual realm. African American psychological adjustment, however, is intricately tied to an understanding that a person's mental well-being is tied to the person's relationship with the divine. The greatest source of support for African Americans has been the church and other religious philosophies. Contemporary therapists have been attempting to integrate this spiritual psychology into modern practice:

> Family therapists, in assessing the strengths and coping skills of Black families, must be sensitive to the role that religion and spirituality play in the lives of many Black people. . . .
>
> Training in the mental health fields largely ignores the role of spirituality and religious beliefs in the development of the psyche and its impact on family life. In the treatment of Black families, this oversight is a serious one.[8]

Dialectic III: The Psychological Dialectic

Racism and African Consciousness: Negation of Respect for and Knowledge of African Traditions   The African style of religious worship maintained the presence of African-based religious practice. The racist denigration of African religion as heathenism left blacks with little recourse but to accept this description or to remain silent. Even though blacks would practice their religion in African ways, blacks in the United States were not allowed to treat their ancestors' religious world with the respect it deserved. This silencing of African traditional religion by American Protestantism left a dynamic absence in the religious consciousness of African Americans that continues to yearn for closure.

The repeated quests to regain, as Long put it, "the image of Africa" throughout African American history reveal that, as in nature, spiritual cultural space abhors a vacuum. This spiritual vacuum of African spirit has led to the movements of Marcus Garvey, the panAfricanism of W. E. B. DuBois, the African dance movement of Katherine Dunham, and, most recently, the Afrocentric movement of cultural black nationalists.

The African collective unconscious continues to urge African Americans to acknowledge their ancestors' presence. While I was driving to a religion conference with a pastor and community activist, a snatch of a poem from T. S. Eliot's *Four Quartets* occurred to me as we crossed the Mississippi River: "The river is full of cargo, chicken coops and dead Negroes."[9] As I recited this line, it was as if I had conjured the presence of our ancestors, whose spirits still were trapped in the mighty Mississippi River. Perhaps they were the hundreds of slaves that didn't make it on the run for freedom from captivity. Perhaps they were the thousands of black bodies who were too weak to make the trip after being "sold down the river." Regardless, my colleague and I both felt a spiritual presence, and we began crying with grief and pledged to be faithful to the memories of our dead ancestors, who still cry out for justice on behalf of their descendants who still carry on in America.

African Americans never have felt secure in celebrating their ethnicity as African people, even though this is very important. African peoples have carried on their cultural traditions and practices by venerating their ancestors. By honoring their ancestors, African people both remember and re-create their cultural space. Until African Americans can remember without shame the pains and joys, the traditions and the practices of their ancestors, they never will be truly free.

Ethnocentrism does not have to mean the negation of other cultural traditions. A healthy ethnocentrism is a form of self-love that can be used to create bridges with other cultures and peoples. Religiously speaking, Christianity should not be posed as an opposite to traditional African religion because they share common historical roots and are not as different as evangelical Christianity led blacks to believe.

In "The Interesting Narrative of Olaudah Equiano, or Gustavus Vassa, the African," a former slave from West Africa wrote about the religious practices of his people. We have this assessment of the religion of his eighteenth-century African community:

> Such is the imperfect sketch, with which my memory has furnished me, of the manners and customs of a people among whom I first drew my breath. And here I cannot forbear suggesting what has long struck me very forcibly, namely, the strong analogy, which, even by this sketch, imperfect as it is, appears to prevail in the manners and customs of my countrymen and those of the Jews, before they reached the Land of Promise, and particularly the Patriarch, while they were yet in that pastoral state which is described in Genesis—an analogy which alone would induce me to think that the one people had sprung from the other.[10]

Even after this relatively positive assessment, Equiano is forced by the prevailing ethos of the day to refer to Africans as "uncivilized and even barbarous," while declaring that Africans are equal to Europeans and did not deserve slavery, that, in fact, God "hath made of one blood all nations of men for to dwell on all the face of the earth" (Acts 17:26).[11]

This silencing and contradictory nature of America's view of African religion has severely limited black Christians' ability to develop a healthy respect for their African cultural traditions. Most often, it has resulted in a silence full of theological possibility waiting to be filled.

Fisher suggested that many of the spirituals not only were African in their style but also were intended to express the slaves' desire to return to Africa.[12] This thesis has yet to be proven conclusively, but there is at least a trace of that desire to come to terms with a lost African homeland in the religious consciousness of black America.

The spirituals have had the power to beckon Americans and Europeans alike to the presence of African religion in Christian guise. The singing of the spirituals by the Fisk Jubilee Singers, Paul Robeson, and opera diva Marian Anderson alerted the white community to what was missing in their own spiritual experiences. The absurdity of existence need not end in hopelessness. The spirituals maintain a sense of pathos and hope amid despair. The spirituals announce that there is another way of bearing the harshest of the realities of modernity in a spiritual dimension that is boundless with possibilities for healing.

> Every time I feel the spirit
> Moving in my heart
> I will pray.
> Every time I feel the spirit
> Moving in my heart
> I will pray.

African American Christianity was born in the crucible of the debates concerning the intellectual, moral, and even human status of Africans. Africans found in the Christian rhetoric of human equality before God an effective voice for their cause that the Declaration of Independence and the Bill of Rights seemed unable to provide. What better way to advance one's own cause than to use the ideology of one's captors?

David Walker's *Appeal* of 1829, probably the first black liberation theology in written form, skillfully presented the case for the liberation of Africans in the United States and throughout the diaspora. Walker's *Appeal* was so powerful that it was banned in the South, and Walker became a marked man, perhaps leading to his mysterious death in 1830.[13]

Walker's choice of the rhetoric of Christian discourse to argue for Africans' freedom signaled a shift in African identity. In this new identity, the African and Christian elements were in creative tension. Walker, like many blacks of that period, was convinced of African Americans' mission to contribute to the "salvation" of Africans. He was proud of his African heritage, and his *Appeal* lobbied for the rights of African nations to exist without European domination.

However, Walker's and other African Americans' acceptance of evangelical Christianity, with its low tolerance and, indeed, outright hostility toward other religious expressions, meant that African Americans had to argue against their own past. Walker's inability to speak in unqualified positive terms about his African religious heritage marks the beginning of both the obscuring and the transforming of the African identity in African Americans. This would lead to an ironic situation, because African American Christianity was to develop in a decidedly different form than its European American counterpart.[14]

The African American community's spoken denial of its African past, while "silently" affirming it by the perpetuation of certain undeniably

African-based practices and beliefs, had a devastating effect on the development of a coherent African American identity and theology. The stillborn attempts to piece together a coherent African American identity have plagued the African American community throughout its existence.

The back-to-Africa movements of black nationalist leaders, including the African nationalism of Marcus Garvey in the early twentieth century and the Rastafarian movement in Jamaica, demonstrate African Americans' desire for a coherent identity in which the African and American parts of the black psyche are honored. DuBois's description of double consciousness is the clearest expression of this social-psychological situation.

The search for a coherent African American identity, however, has not been a concern of African American political and religious leaders alone. Scholars in the fields of family studies and linguistics also have sought to interpret African American behavior in light of West African cultural patterns.[15] African American theologians have been among the last to develop modes of interpretation that include the African past and the African American dialectical identity. African American theologians and religious leaders know only too well how intolerant American Christianity has been toward competing viewpoints, especially when those viewpoints seemed to represent "pagan" manifestations.

The possibility that African Americans could lose their hard-earned civil freedoms because of the charge of paganism is a fear that has some basis. It was common knowledge that even the great liberal Thomas Jefferson saw Africans' morality as deficient. It was his and other liberals' hope that the environment of Euro-American "civilization" eventually would provide Africans with the moral tools for citizenship—a questionable and hypocritical stance since it was slavery, not Africans' religion and culture, that accounted for Africans' problems in the New World. It seems that blaming the victim is not a new social phenomenon in American life.[16]

A Narrative Hermeneutic

The obvious advantage of a narrative hermeneutic is its primary emphasis on the lives and thought of African Americans as told by African Americans. Thus the voices of African Americans are both the sources and the guiding forces behind the interpretation of their religious experiences.

An African American narrative hermeneutic also must show that its particular interpretation is consistent with an African American cultural voice. The narrative perspective that I will be developing pays attention to structural features because of their ability to survive oppressive circumstances over time and because cultures encode their deepest meanings through style or form. Cultures develop different styles of behavior, actions, and attitudes to represent the meanings of that particular culture. These structures, styles, or forms not only are vehicles for the transmission of culture but also represent different modes of orientation and meaning.[17]

In this perspective, form and meaning are inseparable. For example, in African cultures rhythm is especially important in communicating meaning. Structure and meaning are not separate entities; they exist in a dialectical relationship to each other. Cultural styles shape and influence the personal and social lives of their communities. I will show how rhythms are important for the communication of African and African American worldviews. African Americans have utilized African rhythmic styles—and therefore African meanings—in their narrative productions.

This narrative perspective also is influenced by Paul Ricoeur's ideas about the hermeneutics of retrieval. Ricoeur realizes the foundational and liberating nature of narratives:

I would say, borrowing Wittgenstein's term, that the "language-game" of narration ultimately reveals that the meaning of human existence is itself narrative. The implications of narration as a retelling of history are considerable. For history is not only the story (histoire) of triumphant kings and heroes, of the powerful, it is also the story of the powerless and dispossessed. The history of the vanquished dead are crying out for justice demands to be told. . . .

The important point is that the biblical experience of faith is founded on stories and narratives—the story of the exodus, the crucifixion and resurrection, etc.—"before" it expresses itself in abstract theologies which interpret these foundational narratives and provide religious tradition with its sense of enduring identity. The "future" projects of every religion are intimately related to the ways in which it remembers itself.[18]

The realization that stories are the foundation of individual and social identity is essential to the development of a narrative hermeneutic of

African American religion. In the African and African American contexts, oral tradition plays a vital role in the formation of both individuals and community. This oral tradition includes the storytelling and poetry of music. According to linguist Geneva Smitherman:

> Both in slavery times and now, the black community places high value on the spoken word. That community supports a tradition that the anthropologists would call "preliterate." (Although the great Margaret Mead laid the classic bomb on the superiority complex of the Western world when she said that the "influence" of Western culture on non-Western peoples was to make the "preliterate illiterate." In fact, the black oral tradition links Black American culture with that of other oral "preliterate" people—such as Native Americans—for whom the spoken word is supreme.) . . . [F]rom a black perspective, written documents are limited in what they can teach about life and survival in the world. Blacks are quick to ridicule "educated fools," "people who done gone to school and read all dem books and still don't know nothin!" They have "book learning" but no "mother wit," knowledge but not wisdom.[19]

Ricoeur describes some of the ways in which myths have formed and informed Western culture: "Nothing travels more extensively and effectively than myth. Therefore we must conclude that while mythic symbols are rooted in a particular culture, they also have the capacity to emigrate and develop within new cultural frameworks."[20]

This traveling of myths in the American context was a forced journey for African Americans. Africans brought their stories with them in many forms. Stories of the natural and supernatural were brought in the form of folktales, "superstitions," customs, and ways of relating that were a part of the larger cultural story:

> In religion, as in other aspects of their lives, the slaves left a legacy to Americans, black and white, which is still evident. However much debate there is regarding the extent of African survivals, many scholars accept the veracity of the Ashanti proverb, "Ancient things remain in the ears." Although fewer of the ancient African practices and beliefs remained in the ears of American blacks than in the ears of those in Latin America, it was the African memory which made the Afro-Americans a distinctive people. Without Africa and slavery, American folklore, speech, music, literature, cooking, and religion would be unimpressive replicas of European ones, barren and somewhat sterile. Without Africa and slavery, America would not have created spirituals, blues, jazz, or rock and roll. Nor would European immigrants in the Americas ever have escaped from

the constricting tentacles of the sexual repression they inherited from the Middle Ages. In short, Africa and the slave experience are central to an understanding of the American past and present.[21]

The effects of African and African American worldviews on American Christianity seldom have been acknowledged, yet African American Christianity has been and remains a vital religious and political force in America. For African Americans, it provides a distinctive way of being in the world, which, in turn, provides a critical cultural vantage point and sense of personal and social identity.

The Spirituals as Narrative Hermeneutic Principle

African American spirituals are the earliest or one of the earliest narrative representations of the folk religion of the African American people and served as a religious "classic" for the construction of African American religion and theology.[22] Accordingly, spirituals should be a focal point for African American cultural hermeneutics today. African American spirituals were the result of the African American folk community's nascent attempt to come to terms with its forced exile in the New World, under the terms of the prevailing religious ideology of evangelical Christianity, an ideology that African Americans refashioned to express their particular needs and desires.

At one time, historians and theologians concerned with African American religion regarded the spirituals as a fruitful narrative product for study and reflection. A part of the task of our hermeneutic enterprise is to interpret these early interpreters of African American religion. I hope to do this in a way that leads to a clearer understanding of the interpretive process in the study of black religion and culture, using these scholars' commentary on the spirituals as my prime example of this process. The next chapter is an exposition of the nature of the African American spirituals and of the methods employed by their interpreters.

This same kind of narrative hermeneutical analysis also may be done with other "classic" or contemporary forms of African American religion. Worship style, preaching, testimonies, and so on may offer—with varying degrees of success, depending on the quality and amount of material available for study—fresh insights into the theological meanings of African Americans. Other African American cultural forms, including the blues, jazz, and gospel music, also can be used for further investigation into the development and interpretation of African American religious and ethical consciousness.

My examination of the major interpreters of the spirituals will lead to the development of narrative structural and metaphorical categories that I propose as normative points of reference in the analysis of African American religion and culture. This analysis has convinced me of the presence of what have been termed African "survivals," or African structures of meaning that infuse and distinguish the African American religious experience. It is consistent with the findings of anthropologists, linguists, family historians, and literary critics with respect to the nature of African American culture.

Black theologians have seriously neglected the African roots of African American religion. An understanding of how African American religion reflects African religion will become more important as Latin American, Caribbean, and African American Christians increasingly enter into dialogue with their African counterparts about the serious issues of the day, such as the freedom movements in southern Africa. It may be that African and African American theologians have more in common than they now realize and can use that cultural and historical continuity to build programmatic and ideological bridges.

The African American church as a church of liberation and place of survival owes much of its vitality to the presence and preservation of African worldviews. I will show that the structures of the African American spirituals suggest the presence of a theological view whose style is creative (improvisation and spontaneity), communal (call-and-response or antiphonal patterns), and pluralistic (polyrhythms). This style, with its attendant structures of meaning, is infused with an intensely personal faith orientation, which emphasizes a depth of feeling (toward God, humans, and the social situation), a deep desire for freedom, and a strong family bond. The American evangelical tradition permitted the formation of the African American religious tradition, as exemplified by the spirituals.

The structures of the spirituals were formed in the triple dialectic discussed previously, but they also stand in dialectical relationship to each other. These structures reflect an African American religious perspective that is both traditional and empowering for African Americans. For instance, freedom is implicit in African styles of worship. Africans in America needed this cultural style of freedom to help them endure and to create a new "structure of feeling" called African American religion.[23]

The spirituals then become a metaphor or trope that contains and expresses those previously mentioned categories for interpreting African American narrative expressions. We then can speak about African American theology as a "spirituals theology" as long as it reflects these core meanings of creativity, community, and pluralism found in the African American spirituals.

Metaphorical Analysis and Anthropology

The work of cultural anthropologists who have attempted to answer the questions surrounding African and European cultural contact is important. Those anthropologists who have not been blinded by racism or ethnocentrism have provided an intimate look at the religion of Africans as they have come in contact with Europeans on the African continent and in the New World. We will see how the work of Zora Neale Hurston and of Melville Herskovits in African American anthropology and subsequent work by anthropologists of African religion may provide us with methodological insights which can be used in the hermeneutic process.

Although anthropologists of African religion have been more concerned with African religion as it is expressed on the African continent, they also have studied African contact with Christianity and its dialectical transformations in native beliefs and practices. Of particular interest for our purposes is the work of James Fernandez, who has examined African religion and revitalization movements in western, central, and southern Africa and has broadened our knowledge of the process of religious change among African peoples faced with European colonialism, especially through his work on the central African people, the Fang. Here and elsewhere, Fernandez develops a metaphorical method for the study of religious meanings that informs this perspective.

His insights concerning the play of metaphors as a clue to interpretation recall Niebuhr's discussion of the role of metaphors in theological interpretation in *The Responsible Self.* In particular, Fernandez's work on the role of metaphors in religious experience interests us here.[24] Fernandez believes that the key to understanding religion in culture is found in the ways people develop metaphoric clusters of meanings and use these meanings to move them in particular ways. In writing about the Bwiti, he notes that they and other African groups display religious practices that are syncretistic in nature but, most important, are driven by metaphoric action.[25]

Narrative Analysis and Theology

An examination of African American narratives will reveal that their religiosity is defined, empowered, and released when there is a movement of these metaphors in their life situation. The bonds of oppression were resisted by a religious style that emphasized feeling, freedom, and family. This style led to a faith in a personal God who prodded African Americans to develop communities of joy, love, and creativity under the most trying conditions.[26]

The narrative method of this work finds common ground with similar approaches in contemporary theology and cultural anthropology. In the theological realm it shares the interests of narrative theologians who ground their work in the ideas of H. Richard Niebuhr.[27] Niebuhr was concerned that the philosophy of religion be centered in the theological interpretation of the narrative and story of the Christian community. His influential works *The Meaning of Revelation* and *The Responsible Self* lay the groundwork for a narrative that attempts to correlate the social situation with the development of theological meanings.[28]

The Meaning of Revelation attempted to remove the apologetic stance of Christian theology, with its attendant defensiveness and condemnation of other ideas, and move toward a more confessional and pluralistic perspective that sought to discern the movement and activity of God within the context of specific social and historical situations. Niebuhr also called attention to the narrative grounding of the Christian faith. He notes the peculiarly narrative character of Christian origins, as Christianity developed as a series of stories around the central figure of Jesus of Nazareth. Revelation always is historicized and is the product of an interaction between the divine encounter and the human situation.

Niebuhr goes on to suggest that the metaphor of responsibility seems to be emerging in modern culture as a way for Christians to understand their world. He leaves unanswered the question of the relevance of other symbolic forms in Christian interpretation. Niebuhr seems to have been anticipating the pluralism that soon would burst on the contemporary theological scene.[29]

Other theologians have sought to find the meaning of revelation in the human situation and divine encounter, but often there has been a tendency to adopt an apologetic stance in which the Christian revelation must be defended as the truth against other truths. This has been true of neo-orthodox theologians such as Karl Barth and Paul Tillich and also of contemporary narrative theologians like James McClendon and Stanley Hauerwas.[30]

The field of narrative theology would be aided by a consideration of the theoretical perspectives found in the work of selected cultural anthropologists. This consideration would allow the voices of oppressed or marginalized people to be heard and recognized in their particularity and tropic originality. In an article on the role of metaphor, Fitz John Porter Poole points to other theorists, including Lévi-Strauss, who have utilized tropic devices to interpret the meanings of non-Western cultures.[31]

This turn toward the use of metaphor also is gaining influence in the work of historians of religion. Poole mentions the work of Jonathan Z. Smith and his method of "Listenwissenschaft," in which lists of particular features of a culture are compiled to be used in a comparative analysis with different cultures—lists of phenomena as diverse as "Babylonian omens" and "African Ndembu and Yoruba divinations." There is a confluence of perspective as theologians, anthropologists, and historians of religion consider the power of narrative analysis in their respective disciplines.[32]

Unfortunately, narrative theologians have tended to shy away from cultural analysis of metaphors in favor of exploring the possible metaphoric implications of the symbol of Jesus Christ. Niebuhr criticized this aspect of Barth's theological efforts: "The situation of Christians then seems to be this: they cannot understand themselves or direct their actions or give form to their conduct without the use of the symbol Jesus Christ, but with the aid of that symbol only they never succeed in understanding themselves and their values in giving shape to their conduct."³³

Are African American Christians any less Christian because they are able to recognize the presence of symbolic forms and meanings that reflect their African past? Can feminist theologians recover the meanings of goddess worship and use them to inform their Christian theological work and practice? Can Latin Americans employ Marxist thought and symbols and not be thought heretical? Obviously Niebuhr does not provide an answer, but I suggest that the examination of specific cultures—in this case the African American culture—can enrich our understanding of the reality of specific cultural theologies.

Neibuhr's earlier insight that theology never is done in a social or historical vacuum allows us to examine the particularity of Christian theologies as they are influenced by culture, knowing that what we are doing is no different that what Christians always have done.³⁴

Black Literary Theory and Black Religion

African American literary critics, for obvious reasons, have been among those most concerned with African American narration. These scholars have attempted to develop modes of interpretation that are true to African American culture and also to the standards of academic integrity and the art form that is the object of their scrutiny. In chapter 4, I will examine their efforts in the light of the methodological insights of a cultural-structural perspective. While agreeing with the basic intentions of black literary theorists who are attempting to develop a coherent African American narrative hermeneutic, I will demonstrate that they, too, have neglected or distorted the African or African American religious heritage through their reliance on Eurocentric modes of discourse. I will show that some of the earlier black literary theorists, much like W. E. B. DuBois and Hurston, avoided this problem by developing a cultural-structural methodology that recognized the importance of African American religion for black narration.

Black literary theorists have attempted to develop master tropes that reflect the core of African American religion and culture. Houston A. Baker's use of the blues and Henry Louis Gates's use of "signifyin' " are examples. I hope to demonstrate that "spiritual" is a more historically accurate master metaphor for the development and interpretation of black religion and culture.

The Social Context of African American Religion

Finding convictions and solace in the eternal truth of the Christian revelation in its guise as the dominant ideology of Western Europeans is not a luxury that African Americans have been able to enjoy. The Christian faith of African Americans has been fundamentally different, although it shares similar cultural meanings. The cultural situation for African Americans was defined by a social context I term "rapetalistic oppression": the confluence of sexual, economic, and racial oppression. Many of the meanings found in African American spirituals are related to this situation of comprehensive social oppression.

In chapter 6, I will interpret *All God's Dangers: The Life of Nate Shaw* by Theodore Rosengarten.[35] This text enjoys a privileged status in the study of African American culture because it graphically and powerfully depicts the social situation of southern black life and how African American religion played a decisive role in the culture of African Americans.

I believe that by applying the interpretive principles of a theology of the spirituals, attentive to its cultural-structural features, we can gain further insights into the guiding principles that led to the personal and social consciousness of Nate Shaw and produce a new, more adequate interpretation of African American narration.

African American religious experience is an example of the interaction between West African and European modes of thought in which new images and modes of thought became what we know as African American religion, a religion decidedly Christian but also African. I emphasize the African cultural heritage in my analyses of African and African American culture in order to do justice to this neglected side of the cultural dialectic, although I am fully aware of the importance of the Euro-American religious meanings and social context.

A dialectical approach that recognizes the presence of an African religious perspective is essential for a thorough interpretation of African American religion and culture. This view of African American religion as created and reinforced in crisis also may help to explain the intensity of African American religion in its practices of worship, preaching, and music.

While African Americans use prescribed rituals that are part and parcel of the European American cultural heritage, every worship service also becomes a minidrama, a ritualization in which worshipers re-create the new universe of meaning that was developed in the New World encounter between oppressed and oppressor. In this process, the theological meanings are found as much in the structure as they are in the stated meanings. This structure, as I have noted, involves the components of improvisation, call and response or antiphony, and polyrhythms. Through these structures, African Americans are not simply responding to the "hardness" (Long) of their situation or responding only to the "God of the Oppressed" (Cone).[36] Instead, they are responding to the divine presence as they experienced it before the forced pilgrimage to the New World.

The structural analysis I employ is analogous to the interpretation of dreams in the work of Freud in revealing the relationship between manifest and latent meanings. The manifest meanings of the theology may be verbally "Christian," but structurally they are African, giving African American religion its unique style and meaning.[37] This style is what made the difference in the development of an African American religion that produced the beautiful and haunting narrative form known as the spirituals.[38]

The traditional rituals of African Americans were suppressed during slavery in the United States, but in moments of personal and social crisis we see most clearly the preservation of the cultural meanings of Africa. These moments of crisis can be examined and interpreted by employing the insights we gain from the cultural-structural study of the African American spirituals. The life of Nate Shaw will afford an opportunity for just that kind of interpretation.

The work of DuBois is seminal to this study. DuBois's early work on the nature of African American religion utilized a structural dialectical interpretation of African American narrative life. In his classic work, *The Souls of Black Folk,* DuBois employs a narrative style that eminently fits the object of his investigation. This book includes a narrative account of DuBois's observation of an African American worship service, a structural analysis of African American religion, and an interpretation of African American spirituals. DuBois's notion of dialectic informs his well-known concept of the "double consciousness" of African American identity. This concept was DuBois's distinctive and enduring contribution toward an interpretation of African American consciousness. DuBois noted that being an African American was like living in two distinct worlds: one African and the other American. He also used the metaphor of the "veil" to denote the idea of a separation between the lives of Africans and Europeans in America. This separation—as we shall see—was extended into the consciousness of African Americans: "It is a peculiar sensation, this double-consciousness, this sense of always looking at one's self through the eyes of others, of measuring one's soul by the tape of a world that looks on in amused contempt and pity. One ever feels his twoness—an America, a Negro; two souls, two thoughts, two unreconciled strivings; two warring ideals in one dark body, whose dogged strength alone keeps it from being torn asunder."[39]

The most authoritative source for my argument, however, is African American religious experience itself. At any worship service, African Americans still are exhorting their religious leaders, "Tell the story, Preacher! Tell the story!" This story of faith and feeling, family and freedom is better told than written, but writing is the discourse of academia, and so I write.

A Theology of the Spirituals

The Spirituals as Postmodern Discourse

In his autobiographical reflections, Mircea Eliade describes his reactions to a visit to an African American church service:

> One has the impression of being projected into the religious universe of children. The authenticity, the naive realism of the faith that greets you in the Negro spirituals—all that does not belong to the world of adults. One is ushered, as though by enchantment, into a universe that can be imagined only in a dream that certain great poets have glimpsed . . . the passion of the blacks, their nervous instability which makes so many Negro spirituals reach paroxysms of near-hysteria. . . . [H]ere one has the impression that the discovery of the miracle of the Nativity (or other hierophanies) is too elating for the children's souls, and that, finally, the children begin to shout, to clap their hands, to cry for joy, for sadness, for longing. There are so many things to add.[1]

The interpretation of African American religion has been hampered by the social context of American racism and, ironically, by the formation of an African American subculture itself. Is it any wonder, then, that Eliade, perhaps the world's foremost scholar of religions, was puzzled by the phenomenon of African American religion as manifested by African American spirituals? Like many scholars before him, Eliade was both impressed and amazed by this phenomenon. And, like them, he was at a loss to decipher its meaning in the context of the modern world.

This veil has clouded the understanding of African American religion since its conception in the minds and hearts of a captive African people. Many scholars have believed that African American religion was devoid of all meaningful African characteristics or that the Negro church was devoid of a coherent theology.[2]

Only in the past twenty-five years have historians, relying on the testimony of African American captives themselves, produced more satisfying attempts at the historical reconstruction of African American religion.[3] These scholars have allowed readers a more comprehensive understanding of the dialectical nature of African American religion. This historical reconstruction should have had a profound influence on the development of African American theology, but, unfortunately, it has been largely ignored by black theologians and ethicists, who have been slow to incorporate these historical investigations into their theological paradigms. African American theologians have been too quick to follow American and European theological paradigms that stress abstract philosophical rather than historical data as theological starting points.[4]

This problem is not only a matter of the use of historical information; it also has to do with the racist ideology that has distorted the perception of African Americans by African Americans. Racist ideology in the United States has caused African American religious interpretation to undergo a dialectical process, which I refer to as the ethnocentric dialectical process in African American theological thought. In this dialectical process, European American Protestant ethnocentrism lent force to a narrow monotheism that labeled non-European religions as "heathen" or false, with no redeeming value.

This ethnocentric dialectical movement led African American Christians to deny—even to themselves—the positive aspects of their African-based religion. This stands in sharp contrast to European Christians who still honor and study their own "pagans," such as Socrates, Plato, and many other pre-Christian thinkers. The "polytheism," militarism, and many other social differences of their "heathen" ancestors do not prevent philosophers and theologians alike from basing much of their intellectual work on their paradigms.

Western Christianity itself is a synthesis of distinctively Christian, Hebraic, and Hellenistic thought. This synthesis, however, has received the dominant culture's stamp of approval and does not have to bear the weight of being labeled syncretistic or pagan. It is privileged by virtue of its powerful position in the society.

African Americans practiced their African-influenced religion in order to survive in a racist culture, but they were not allowed to name it as both African and Christian. In a society that denigrated all things black and African, doing so would have been tantamount to political, economic, and social suicide. This ethnocentric dialectic was insidious because it seemingly was self-imposed. Racist and ethnocentric ideology became internalized, and the contribution of African culture to African American Christianity in the United States was obscured. Any embracing of this "heathen" past would have been a political liability for African Americans attempting to gain acceptance in the mainstream of American social life. The quest for black political rights often has been linked with the black community's willingness or ability to conform to the standards of a Christianity that embodied European norms of civilization. African American religious practitioners and theologians had to be careful, therefore, to suppress any positive references to their African religious heritage.

Even David Walker, one of the earliest and strongest advocates of black nationalism, felt compelled to adopt a critical attitude toward the practice of "pagan" African religion. This distinction also is found in one of the earliest and most powerful African slave narratives, the narrative of Olaudah Equiano (Gustavus Vassa). Even though Equiano was proud of his African religious heritage, we can see the development of a narrative strategy that attempted to skirt or blunt this issue. Equiano adopted the ethnocentric evangelical Christian faith of the early American period, with its rhetoric of disdain for "pagan" religious practices. Nevertheless, he offered a sympathetic account of his native African village's religious and cultural practices, an account that, for that period, amounted to a ringing endorsement of African religious life. Yet Equiano could not explicitly endorse traditional African religion because of the tenor of the times, which required that any respectable Christian— or any Westerner, for that matter—look upon heathen (including Jewish) religious practices with disdain.[5]

This theological problem, then, also is one that concerns the production of ideology. Blacks have been forced to defend their humanity and religious practices in the context of racist America by adopting the rhetorical strategy of their Christian oppressors and liberators. They were forced to defend their religious practices against a prevailing racist ideology and an equally oppressive ethnocentric religious ideology.

African Americans were accused either of being bad imitators of American Christianity or of practicing a heathen form of Christianity. Unable to set the terms of the debate, blacks were trapped into defending themselves against one or the other of these accusations. Neither alternative could lead to a positive evaluation of the African nature of their African American religious practices. Africans in the New World— reluctantly at first, as seen in the case of Equiano, and later more enthusiastically in Walker—chose to defend themselves from charges of heathenism by adopting the prevailing notions of African religious inferiority.

The powerful forces of racism in the late nineteenth and earlier twentieth century also led blacks to adopt a socially defensive stance as the church became the only place where African Americans could feel safe to express their sense of social and religious identity. This defensive stance of the black church has been attacked by scholars who argued that it was proof of the otherworldly and inconsequential role of the black church in the African American freedom movement. Recent work in dialectical theory, however, has reminded us that oppressed persons demonstrate their resistance to the status quo through the development of distinctive cultural styles.[6]

Some blacks, mainly those of a burgeoning middle class, sought to imitate American mainstream forms of religious practice during this time. But the black lower classes' secular and sacred communities produced new forms of worship, music, and religious practice that demonstrated that blacks were in the process of developing and maintaining an identity and value system separate from their oppressors. The rise of the blues, gospel music, and pentecostalism are examples of the cultural and religious resistance in which African Americans were engaged while they faced an intransigent and increasingly hostile social environment.[7]

Recent work by Iain MacRobert on the origins of pentecostalism in the black church reveals the role of African religion in the creation of a new form of African American religion. MacRobert cites Hollenwegers's identification of the "black roots" of pentecostalism as orality of liturgy, narrativity of theology and witness, maximum participation resulting in a reconciliatory form of community, dreams and visions, and body-mind relationships that reveal principles of correspondence as seen in healing by prayer.[8]

MacRobert demonstrates the cultural-structural dialectic nature of African American pentecostal religion, in which African and African American meanings cocreated a new religious practice:

> Not only did the motor behavior of the participants reveal the early Pentecostal movement's debt to African folk religion, but the leitmotive of black Christianity, which had their origins either in Africa or in slavery, continued to echo in early black inspired Pentecostalism: Spirit possession and spiritual power (accompanied by trances, dreams, prophesying, healing and exorcism); the integration of the seen and unseen worlds; freedom; racial equality; black personhood and dignity; community; and belief in the imminent Second Advent of Christ. . . . The relevance and integration of religion and the supernatural in all of life and the joyous celebration of life was expressed in forms of liturgy which originated in West Africa. The African desire and respect for spiritual power and belief in Spirit possession was central to the movement. . . . This possession took place to the accompaniment of music, dancing and motor behavior which was essentially West African in origin. The immanence of God was recognized and the power and presence of God experienced in the liberty of the Spirit. Western literary theology was displaced by the oral theology of the story, the testimony and the song.[9]

The present study builds on the work of scholars, like MacRobert, who interpret African American religion as a dialectical process in which the beliefs of traditional African religions and evangelical Christianity and the situation of racist oppression interacted to form African American religion.

In the African situation, where the traditional African cultural characteristics of the religion are more obvious, many religious groups continue to practice traditional African rituals alongside Euro-Christian practices. In the African American situation, however, the African aspects of African American religion have been maintained through unnamed and unclaimed forms and styles of religious practice. These styles continue to give specific African meanings to African American religion.

This leads to a central problem in theological method in considering African American religion. In its American and European forms, theology has been part and parcel of the dialogue of the socially and politically powerful. The voices of the oppressed have not received serious attention. Classic works in American theology assume a Eurocentric view of the world. Works such as Reinhold Niebuhr's *The Nature and Destiny of Man* and Paul Tillich's *Systematic Theology* view Christianity from a European philosophical perspective. The religious ideas and practices of culturally and socially marginal groups simply have not been part of the conversation.[10]

Theologians concerned with African American religion must use different tools and listen to different stories for their theological exposition. The traditional tools of philosophical and systematic theology presume the historicity of European development and colonization. This historical past includes the assumption of a desacralized, scientific universe—a view that is not consistent with African American views of the world.

The stance I advocate for this task belongs to the purview of narrative hermeneutics. What is needed is an interpretive perspective that examines and interprets the narratives of particular cultural groups in order to explicate their particular theological meanings within the context of their culture and history. If revelation is not to be the privilege of the socially and politically powerful who control the modes of discourse, then theologians of the black experience must search for instances of revelation in their own cultural texts. Although this has been the stated intent of black theologians since the work of Benjamin Mays in the 1930s, as we saw, this stated intent often has yielded to a Eurocentric perspective in terms of sources or methods.

Spirituals are perhaps the earliest African American narrative religious products. They surely are the most studied of all African American religious forms. In my examination of the recent historiography of African American religion, I have demonstrated the African cultural heritage of the spirituals in particular and African American religion in general. My hope is to demonstrate the need for and effectiveness of a dialectical narrative hermeneutic of African American religion. This narrative hermeneutic must be cultural-structural in method and dialectical, in that it must understand African American religion as the production of cultural, political, and ethnocentric dialectical forces.

As we will see in chapter 4, developing an adequate narrative hermeneutic in part is a response to African American literary critics who also have adopted Western hermeneutical theories in their attempts to develop a coherent black literary theory. I hope to show that African

American culture and thought must be the foundation of an adequate African American narrative hermeneutic.

Cultural-Structural Method: Form, Meaning, and Metaphor

The question of the implicit meanings in African American religion as found in the spirituals will revolve around questions of methodology in the interpretation of African American religion and culture. Methodology becomes extremely important because of the subordinate social and political situation of African Americans. The world of African Americans was not the taken-for-granted world of the society at large. Therefore, attempts to treat African American religion and culture as clear, unambiguous phenomena are doomed to failure.

Attempts to examine African American religion with theoretical tools that assume European norms are fated to distort the religious meanings of African Americans. These tools presuppose the presence of cultural universals, although in reality these often are specifically Anglo-American cultural forms. This does not mean that all established academic tools must be excluded. However, it privileges dialectical methods that recognize the interconnectedness of structure, form, and meaning.

Form is not the only way in which theological meanings are expressed in African American religious experience. African American religion is replete with central metaphors that carry the most deeply held beliefs of the community. These metaphors, as we shall see, also reflect a dialectical process that includes the African and the African American situations.[11]

A relatively adequate theological method for African American religion, then, would include the identification and interpretation of these master or central metaphors that tell us about the core beliefs of the African American community. A narrative analysis also would attend to the ways that meaning has been encoded in structures and forms. This interpretive procedure would give us an interpretation of the overall style or theological orientation of the African American religious community.

Seen as an early form of communication between African American community members and their divine world, the spirituals give us special insight into the early definitive structuring of the African American religious community. In the spirituals, the members of the community testified to each other about their hopes, wishes, fears, and beliefs. They spoke about those things that made central differences in their lives. Their forms of address, replete with metaphors of family, were symbols for their ideas of their relationship to the divine and human community.

Black theologians have been more successful at identifying the central political metaphoric themes, what I term the political dialectic, but often pay insufficient attention to the cultural situation out of which these metaphors arose. A recognition of the social and cultural contexts would serve to expand and deepen these scholars' interpretation of the spirituals.

Cultural/Structural Model One: W. E. B. DuBois

Beginning with W. E. B. DuBois, many scholars have sought the central meanings of African American religion in the spirituals. DuBois viewed the spirituals, or sorrow songs, as he called them, as an unequaled African American and American cultural achievement:

> Little of beauty has America given the world save the rude grandeur God himself stamped on her bosom; the human spirit in this new world has expressed itself in vigor and ingenuity rather than in beauty. And so by fateful chance the Negro folksong—the rhythmic cry of the slave—stands today not simply as the sole American music, but as the most beautiful expression of human experience born this side of the seas. It has been neglected, it has been, and is, half despised, and above all it has been persistently mistaken and misunderstood; but notwithstanding, it still remains as the singular spiritual heritage of the nation and the greatest gift of the Negro people.[12]

DuBois also asserted the influence of Africa in African American religion in his discussion of the three features of African American religion: the preacher, the music, and the frenzy.[13] DuBois called the preacher the "most unique personality developed by the Negro on American soil. A leader, a politician, an orator, a 'boss,' an intriguer, an idealist,—all these he is, and ever, too, the centre of a group of men, now twenty, now a thousand in number."[14] DuBois traces the priest back through the slavery of the Americas to his first incarnation as the priest in African village life.[15]

Music also is important to the religious life of African Americans. DuBois calls the music of Negro religion the "most original and beautiful expression of human life and longing yet born on American soil. Sprung from the African forests, where its counterpart can still be heard, it was adapted, changed, and intensified by the tragic soul-life of the slave, until, under the stress of law and whip, it became the one true expression of a people's sorrow, despair, and hope."[16] Although DuBois has a tendency to refer to only the melancholic aspects of the spirituals, in this passage he recognizes that this music also can be the vehicle for hope as well as sorrow. Sorrowful hope may be the most accurate characterization of DuBois's interpretation of the Negro spirituals. Last, DuBois discussed the "frenzy":

> Finally the Frenzy of "shouting," when the Spirit of the Lord passed by, and, seizing the devotee, made him mad with supernatural joy, was the last essential of Negro religion and the one more devoutly believed in than all the rest. It varied in expression from the silent rapt countenance or the low murmur and moan to the mad abandon of physical fervor,— the stamping, shrieking, and shouting, the rushing to and fro and wild waving of arms, the weeping and laughing, the vision and the trance.[17]

DuBois emphasizes that for generations many blacks "believed that without this visible manifestation of the God there could be no true communion with the Invisible."[18] For DuBois, these three themes of the preacher, the music, and the frenzy constitute the major features of African American religion. All are descendants of African traditional religion. DuBois even goes so far as to relate the frenzy to the ancient oracular manifestations of Delphi and Endor.[19] This placed frenzy— probably the most "heathenish" feature of African American religion— on a par with classical religious expressions and gave an elegant status to a much-maligned feature of black religion.

In the final chapter of the *Souls of Black Folk,* DuBois discusses the African origin and dialectical nature of African American religion. He identifies three phases of the development of African American spirituals: those spirituals that are directly related to African musical styles, those songs that are African American, and those songs that blend African American music with European American styles.[20]

DuBois also identifies some of the themes present in the music of the slaves: an emphasis on the power of God, the presence of natural elements, the pain of forced bondage, the hope for freedom and novelty, and the cry for mother and child. DuBois also was astute enough to note that even the absence of certain themes, such as fatherhood and the experience of marriage, connoted something important about the life-world of the slaves.

DuBois concluded that hope was the central meaning of these sacred songs, a hope that was founded in a faith in the ultimate justice of the divine. This justice could manifest itself in life, death, or a world beyond this one. In the concluding words of this essay and the book itself, DuBois interpreted the style and substance of these songs in political terms: Africans in America sang to express their desire for freedom.[21]

Although DuBois does not offer an extended discussion of the metaphors of justice, family, creativity, nature, and faith in a powerful God, he nevertheless reveals a deep sensitivity to both the African and the African American forms and themes of African American religion. He applied to African American narratives a cultural-structural dialectical methodology that sought to uncover and identify structural features and themes of African American religious meanings as they related to African religion or African American religion. DuBois's work in the interpretation of the spirituals is important because it should have served as a methodological paradigm for future work in the study of African American religion.

Instead of building on the work of DuBois, however, most subsequent theological interpreters of African American religion have ignored this methodology, which would have given a more accurate cultural and historical interpretation of African American religion. Black theologians have claimed to interpret African American religion by using the narrative sources of blacks, but they largely have ignored DuBois's work and, instead, have employed methods that have yielded culturally ambiguous results.

Social scientists and historians relied on the cultural-structural methodology that DuBois developed. This has resulted in these scholars' recognition of the African and American cultural dialectical heritage of African American religion as an important factor in understanding that religion.

Perhaps those closest to a phenomenon have the most difficulty seeing it objectively. The political climate of Christian America, which denigrated African beliefs and customs, may have placed black religionists in an apologetic mode that required a defense of African American religion to the detriment of its African cultural heritage. Even DuBois, the father of the Pan-African movement among American blacks, was influenced by the negative portrayals of African culture. His portrayal of African American religion in its early stages is replete with images of exorcism, weird midnight orgies, witchcraft, and the sacrifice of human victims. This popular image of African religion was based on European American Christian notions and bore little relationship to the life-world of most African people:

> He called up all the resources of heathenism to aid,—exorcism and witch-craft, the mysterious Obi worship with its barbarious rites, spells, and blood-sacrifice even, now and then, of human victims. Weird midnight orgies and mystic conjurations were invoked, the witch-woman and the voodoo-priest became the centre of Negro group life, and that vein of vague superstition which characterizes the unlettered Negro even to-day was deepened and strengthened.[22]

Cultural-Structural Model Two:
Zora Neale Hurston

DuBois's interpretation of the spirituals was challenged by Zora Neale Hurston, who helped to sharpen our understanding of the spirituals and of African and African American culture. Hurston is critical of DuBois's designation of the spirituals as "sorrow songs," concluding: "The idea that the whole body of spirituals are 'sorrow songs' is ridiculous. They cover a wide range of subjects from a peeve at gossipers to Death and Judgement."[23] She also notes the improvisational nature of the spirituals and the fact that they are "unceasing variations around a theme."[24] This is a theme in which feeling itself is the central meaning: "The nearest thing to a description one can reach is that they are Negro religious songs, sung by a group, and a group bent on expression of feelings and not on sound effects."[25]

Hurston continues her structural analysis of the spirituals and attempts to make her readers aware that the spirituals they have heard in concert bear little resemblance to the original spirituals of black folk religion. She emphasizes the unique style of the spirituals as an important part of their meaning: The jagged style, the dissonances, the breaks in melody and key are important, since no two performances of a spir-

itual by the congregation will be alike. Through this musical improvisation, the congregation expresses its mood for the day.[26]

Hurston's analysis reveals several structural characteristics of the spirituals. In addition to intense feeling, there is a play of different pitches
and keys so that feelings guide the creation of the music. The structure
is inherently pluralistic and is guided not by rules of orderly composition
and production but by the communal spirit and individual feelings of
the moment of performance. This is a religious form in which the
deepest emotional needs of the community find expression. It is an
experience marked by communal interplay and responsiveness.

Hurston, in even stronger and more unequivocal terms than DuBois,
was convinced of the African nature of African American religion. She
was convinced that the spirituals were a form of cultural resistance
against European American cultural and religious norms for the interpretation of African American religious and cultural life. The ethnocentric dialectic would have no place in the work of Zora Neale Hurston.

In the sanctified church, the presence of African rhythms and dancing
are expressions of a cultural resistance against the Europeanization or
Americanization of African American religion and culture. The Negro
churches' ready acceptance of European American forms of worship,
especially their reliance on European American musical styles, is resisted
by African Americans of the lower social classes, who still express their
Christianity in a different, more Africanized style that also was the mark
of the spirituals.

Hurston also sees African spirit possession and the African American
churches' emphasis on being filled with the spirit as equivalent forms.
She is convinced that the sanctified African American church is a continuation of African religion on American shores.[27]

Hurston's structural analysis interprets African American religious experience in terms of a cultural dialectical synthesis of African and African
American religion.. Later commentators also have come to mark as a
feature of its African predecessor the idea that Negro religion is based
on rhythm. Such noted anthropologists of African religion as Herskovits,
Robert Farris Thompson, and Noel King subsequently gave credence to
the importance of dance in African religion.[28]

A pluralistic communal environment in which the preacher and the
congregation interact in a call-and-response pattern and the phenomenon of possession particularly reflect African religion. Instead of focusing

only on the stated meanings, Hurston realizes that structures also carry meanings and that these meanings are continuous with an African religious heritage.

Hurston's comments reflect the cultural dialectic. She has important things to say about the African cultural basis of African American religion, and she rebuts the ethnocentric dialectic with her strong affirmation of African-based religions. Her work has less to say about the political nature of black religion.

Hurston wrote her comments on the spirituals during the 1930s, when she was a research student of Franz Boas, one of the founders of American anthropology who did much to combat the racist uses of anthropology. Hurston never completed her graduate studies and, instead, went on to become one of the most important African American novelists and writers of her day. The failure of scholars of religion to recognize the importance of her works, even in passing, may be the result of a latent sexism in American religious scholarship or an over-reliance on traditional scholarly approaches.[29]

Cultural-Structural Model Three: Melville Herskovits

Melville Herskovits, a contemporary of DuBois and Hurston, provided some of the most extensive reasons for arguing that African American religion was not simply a debased imitation of European American Christianity. In his classic work, *The Myth of the Negro Past,* Herskovits argues for a cultural continuity between African and African American religion. In Herskovits's discussion of the spirituals, he recounts some of the debates about the origin of the spirituals and discounts arguments that the spirituals were not of African American origin. He does this by comparing the structure of the spirituals with songs found in West African cultures and finds the style and form of African American religion to be almost identical with West African musical patterns and styles.[30]

These West African cultural structural elements of improvisation, call and response, and diverse or polyphonic rhythms also were mentioned in Hurston's discussion of the African American spirituals. Herskovits's structuralist method, which attends to cultural similarities between West African and African American cultural products, demonstrates this cultural linkage. This relationship is so strong that even those who have disagreed with the idea of cultural continuity between West African and African American culture acknowledge this cultural-structural similarity.

Herskovits's analysis is similar to that of Hurston and DuBois in embracing the cultural relationship between African and African American religion. Like Hurston, he has less to say about the political nature of black religion.

Hurston based her interpretation of the African nature of religion on a cultural-structuralist dialectical methodology in which cultural forms are the determinating factor in the interpretive process. What we have, then, are three authors who agree on the African nature of African American religion. DuBois is more influenced by the political and ethnocentric dialectic view of African American religion, which gives his analysis a sharp political critique with a more balanced appraisal of the influence of African religion on the development of African American religion. DuBois may have been concerned that the Negro never would be accepted or advance in modern society as long as African religious views led whites to exclude African Americans from participation in the modern world.

African Ritual Structure and African American Religion

DuBois and Hurston were concerned especially with the role of feeling in African American religion. In their work, we find the enunciation of structures that were constituent of African American religion. DuBois and Hurston outlined a ritual structure that later anthropologists explicated in their ethnography of African religions. Students of anthropology immediately will recognize this structural style of liminality and communitas in Victor Turner's discussion of African ritual performance.[31] In a text on the anthropology of the Tshidi, a southern African people, Jean Comaroff mentions how Victor Turner, the celebrated anthropologist of African religion, developed the idea of "permanent liminality" which was associated with the desire for "communitas." This idea of *permanent* liminality—as distinguished from regular liminality, which occurred during particular rites of passage—suggests a spiritual state in which a worshiping community continually is enacting rituals that give it a quality of, as Turner called it, "anti-structure," or what Comaroff terms "counter-structure." The difference in their views is that Comaroff is more aware of religious rituals as a dialectically based, socially transformative practice.[32]

DuBois and Hurston's depiction of rural African Americans' performance of the spirituals in language that suggests a mysterious ritual quality, by which the congregants are creating a world that is totally alien to the one in which they are entrapped, is a precursor to Turner's ideas of African worship as a series of ritual events that create a cultural space different from normal cultural activity (liminality), which eventually leads to a strengthening of the community's sense of social solidarity and union (communitas).

In performing the spirituals, African Americans are free to be spontaneous and improvisational, to engage in call and response, to be polyrhythmic, and to show intense feelings in a setting that is set apart from their everyday existence. These liminal activities—which were suppressed and discouraged by the ruling order—now are given free expression as worshipers gather to express themselves in cultural ways that are antistructural or counterstructural to the dominant order.

DuBois and Hurston emphasized the role of music and of priestly figures in black religion. DuBois focused on the preacher in the institutional black church, while Hurston examined the role of the "hoodoo doctors" in black folk religion. Like many social scientists of their day, DuBois and Hurston were interested in describing the patterns of non-Western cultures.[33]

Their methods did not occur in a vacuum. They were the products of and contributors to contemporary sociological and anthropological methods. The great sociologist Max Weber was an admirer of DuBois's *The Souls of Black Folk* and asked DuBois's permission to arrange for its translation for a German audience.[34]

DuBois and Hurston were trained by leading figures in the development of the modern social sciences. What I have termed their cultural-structural method is similar to Webster's methodologies and reflect procedure of establishing ideal types that could serve as measuring rods for social behavior. However, like modern anthropologists, they also were interested in showing distinctive patterns of behavior in the African American community.[35]

They did not view these differences ipso facto as evidence of cultural deficiency. They shared the desire of some of their fellow social scientists to demonstrate the "normality" of non-Western cultures because of the sustained critique of these peoples by Enlightenment and post-Enlightenment writers. Hurston's mentor Franz Boas was a leading figure in American anthropology who almost singlehandedly debunked notions of the biological racial inferiority of non-Western peoples.[36]

However, they differed from Weber and Boas in being the subjects of their own investigations. They were not just participant-observers; they were participating-observers. They realized that they were, in DuBois's terminology, the victims of double-consciousness, the phenomenon in which they experienced psychological distress because of the larger society's notions of the differences of African Americans as deficiencies. In this situation, a person feels torn between two different but interrelated realities.

DuBois and Hurston developed different ways of dealing with this social fact: DuBois through his political advocacy and Hurston through her literary depictions of black life. Nevertheless, both realized the importance of accurately rendering and interpreting African Americans' behavior in light of their African cultural heritage. Interestingly, Herskovits provides an intellectual link between this early period of cultural structuralism and the modern period, in which narrative analysis provides further insights into the study of culture. DuBois, Hurston, and Herskovits all wrote before the recent advances in linguistics and narrative theory.

James W. Fernandez, who was Herskovits's last doctoral student and who received the Melville Herskovits Award in Cultural Anthropology for his work in the anthropology of African religion, employed a narrative strategy of metaphors.[37] His work builds on Herskovits's earlier concern for accurate description by examining the central patterns through metaphoric analysis.

I do not mean to suggest that DuBois and Hurston agreed on all aspects of black religion and culture because they shared similar methodological styles that centered on the identification of the central metaphors and style of African American religion and culture. For instance, Hurston disagreed with DuBois's characterization of the spirituals as "sorrow songs" and with his belief that truth and beauty should be linked in the political program for black advancement. She was more willing to show the foibles of the folk in their sublime human responses.[38]

But DuBois and Hurston both presented African American culture as a complex and elegant community production. The danger with recent advances in cultural theory is that the people under study may be lost in the explication of the cultural text, which is understood as subjectless and governed by "universal rules" of interpretation. I will say more about this in chapter 4. DuBois and Hurston interpreted the particular forms they found in African American religion as manifestations of universal forms, as in the case of frenzy and feeling, but they did so without losing respect for the unique ways in which these characteristics appeared in African American cultural life. In most cases, they recognized that differences are the hallmarks of culture, and they neither romanticized those differences nor denied their reality in the cultural life of African Americans.

The Spirituals and Postmodern Discourse

Spirituals are, above all else, a cultural style. They are a cultural practice in which the spirit of African ancestors has been coded, transformed, and passed down from generation to generation. Zora Neale Hurston was absolutely correct: Spirituals are being created every day in the African American community. Spirituals are not a set body of songs with a sacred canon of songs, known and unknown; they are a cultural style by which Africans in America continually have expressed their deepest joys and sorrows. Every time a black mother moans over the death or injury of her son, she is creating a spiritual. Every time a black father cries over the lost potential of a daughter's wasted life he is living a spiritual. Spirituals are living entities within the African American community. They wear different guises, but their performance is the same. They take sorrow and work with it until it becomes a shout of joy. They create praise from pain, despite the bleakness of black life in America.

The ancestral themes that were born during slavery still have power in the African American community. These themes are the bones of conjuration used to produce spiritual power. Faith in the divine presence is most powerfully experienced when family and freedom are at risk.

This depth of feeling acts as a bottomless reservoir upon which feeds the anguish of black pain, as more and more of black America's children experience the urban crises of drugs, unemployment, and crime. Spirituals—that is, the strength and presence of the ancestors—stand ready to provide new generations of black Americans hope in the midst of despair.

In modern academic language, the spirituals are the black community's postmodern response to the oppression of modernity. Historically speaking, Africans were taken captive during the development of Europe's modern period. Hassan[39] offers a useful chart of modernist and postmodernist characteristics that illustrates the cultural aesthetic sensibility of Europe's modernist period. I will reproduce only those pairs that make my point about the postmodern status of spirituals.

Cultural Styles

Modernism	Postmodernism
form	antiform
purpose	play
hierarchy	anarchy
mastery/logos	exhaustion/silence
art object/finished work	process/performance/happening
distance	participation
centering	dispersal
selection	combination
master code	idiolect
genital/phallic	polymorphous/androgynous
origin/cause	difference-difference/trace
God the Father	the Holy Ghost
determinacy	indeterminacy
transcendence	immanence

Even though postmodernism sounds like a historical category, in reality it is a style of being in the world.[40] The example of postmodernism in literature referred to most often is the essay form made popular by Montaigne in the sixteenth century. In these essays, Montaigne championed the cause of humanism and a respect for disparate cultures.

Modernism has been a movement in Western culture synonymous with the development of literacy and writing as the dominant mode of communication.[41] This push for logocentrism as embedded in the written word has been a hallmark of the development of Western civilization. Those cultures that retained their oral nature, with its subsequent antimodern worldview, were deemed less worthy of respect by Westerners. African American spirituals stand as testimony by their African creators as an antimodern or postmodern response to a modernism that helped to produce the situation of African captivity in America.

African captives in America by and large were not allowed to read or write. Therefore, their cultural texts had to be based on oral traditions. Their style, which could be "read" only through the performance of their oral narratives, encoded the deep meanings of the message. In this tradition, the words were important, but the sound of the words was more important still.

The spirituals had to be sung with the feeling of the life that was being lived. When the community was happy, spirituals sounded happy. When the community was distraught, spirituals carried that message. When freedom was contemplated, spirituals carried the message of impending liberation. Each person could put his or her own consciousness into the sound that was being produced. Moans and wails coexisted with shouts of joy and exaltation.

A Sounding Religion

Words as the vehicles for sounds, rather than sounds as the vehicles for words, reversed the logocentric order of modern understandings of language, as African captives reproduced the sounds of their forgotten languages in the words and sentences of their captors' language. The rhythms of the performance of the spirituals communicated the state of mind of the individual or the participants. Slower rhythms indicated sadness, a deep sense of reverence, or simply an invocation and call to worship. Faster rhythms indicated that the Holy Ghost had arrived and was moving through the community. Memories of dead ancestors— those adults or children lost through death, the auction block, or escape—were revived as the community sought to exorcise the demons of despair by honoring the memories of their beloved community.

Rhythms gave way to polyrhythms, as each member contributed his or her own beat to the cacophony of sound. The language of sounds was punctured by shouts of "Praise God," "Thank you, Jesus," "My

Lord," and "Help me." Spontaneity was the only rule as worshipers improvise in voice, words, and movements that convey the innermost feelings of joy and sorrow. Form gave way to antiform, hierarchy to anarchy, distance to participation, transcendence to immanence, and finally mastery to exhaustion and silence as the play of spirits finally ceased and souls found rest and strength to begin another day.

The Holy Ghost

African American religion based on spirituals emphasizes the role of the Holy Ghost. This creative and prophetic aspect of the godhead has been the most prominent feature of African American religion. Beginning in the African homeland, where all the world was seen as capable of reflecting the presence of the spirit, African captives found the revivalist religion of eighteenth- and nineteenth-century religion a perfect foil for the expression of this spirit.

It is ironic that this reliance on the spirit also led to the development of pentecostalism in the twentieth century. Black religion rightfully can lay claim to being the author of many new religious movements in the twentieth century, the greatest of which is the pentecostal movement that has become a worldwide phenomenon, claiming the allegiance of millions of adherents in the Americas and around the globe.[42] The Azusa Church revival of 1904 spawned a religious movement based on the direct experience of the Spirit through the Baptism of the Holy Spirit and the speaking of unknown tongues. Racism, that most traditional of American spiritual phenomena, eventually led to a splitting of this movement into separate racial camps. However, this postmodern emphasis on the Holy Ghost was captured in the development of African American religion.

The emphasis on the Spirit did not stop with the pentecostal movement. The creative activity of the Holy Ghost was at work in the development of numerous religious movements and artistic styles in the black community during this black immigration from South to North. The creation of Muslim religious groups—the Nation of Islam, the Moorish Science Temple, the Black Hebrews—as well as numerous other religious groups such as the Spiritualist churches and the movements of Father Divine, Daddy Grace, and Sister Catharine, revealed the creative activity of the spirit in African American religion.

During this time, mainstream black middle-class churches, Baptists and Methodists, were heading toward acceptance in a modern world. In so doing, they left the poorer and even more marginalized black community members to fend for themselves. The mainstream black church's refusal to open its arms to gospel music because it was deemed too "worldly" was symptomatic of this attitude. This, however, did not prevent other religious groups—notably pentecostal and those black churches of less power and prestige, like the Spiritualists—from championing this new religious creation that appealed to the masses of black folk. This appeal was so strong that these same middleclass black churches eventually were forced to embrace it, lest they lose any hope of reaching future black generations.

This postmodern style, which first was developed in America in African American spirituals, continued to express itself in gospel music, despite the middle-class black community's attempt to fit into a modern paradigm, with its emphasis on order and hierarchy.

It is no wonder that many of these black religious movements also returned religious leadership to black women because women had been relegated to secondary roles in the black Baptist and Methodist churches.[43] Before and during captivity, African women were priestesses and diviners of spirits. Toni Morrison's *Beloved* provides an excellent portrait of the spiritual leadership exercised by black women during the days of captivity. Slave narratives also give witness to the continual call of the Holy Ghost to black women, many of whom exercised their religious leadership despite the protests of men.[44]

Always Already   African American religion based on the spirituals is a religious experience that is always already happening. It is continually creative and changing its nature and form. Yet its style remains consistent with its African cultural foundations. Spirituals give way to gospel; gospel gives way to contemporary gospel; contemporary gospel gives way to pop gospel and rap—but the style that features improvisation, call and response, and polyrhythms remains the same.

The restless spirits of African ancestors continually seek ways of announcing their presence by silencing previous forms. The passage of time creates absences that stimulate the creative activity of spirit, and new forms emerge that carry the same postmodernist structural features that were described by historians of African and African American religion and culture.

Play

This spirit of improvisation has ancient African roots. In an article describing ancient Nubia's cultural play on its powerful Egyptian counterpart, two archaeologists describe its unique artistic process to a reporter in this way:

> "It becomes a very spontaneous art, full of free-flowing improvisation," she said, pausing before a Meroitic pot. "You see that?" She pointed to a curling snake painted on the vessel, holding in its mouth a drooping flower. "The flower is obviously an ankh."
>
> I gasped in sudden recognition. I had seen many an ankh on Egyptian objects: a cross-shaped symbol topped with an oval, which is the hieroglyph for the verb "to live." In Egyptian art, the ankh appears alone or in rows of declarative rigidity. On the Meroitic pot, the snake stings the world to life with a flower. "The Egyptians are too staid for this. . . . They don't like loopy things."
>
> . . . In Egypt, . . . the ba statue, which represents a dead person's spirit, is a formal-looking bird with a human head; in Meroe, the ba becomes a human with wings. The pots dance with two-legged crocodiles, with giraffes ranging from the lordly to the comic, with deer darting through shadows. There are abstract designs made of endless waves of draped festoons and floral curlicues.
>
> The sheer exuberance of Meroitic art proclaims a civilization that believed in pleasure and playfulness. The pots were largely used for wine drinking. At certain Meroitic sites, whole barrooms have been excavated.[45]

This obviously is a culture that understood the value of play. Its postmodern features are evident as the Nubian artists sought to deconstruct the rigid posturing of their imperialistic Egyptian cousins to the north. This playfulness within African cultures is an important advisory against a naive nativistic monolingual view of African religion and culture. The dialectical play of the postmodern spirit is continually threatened by a modern view that features control and hierarchy.

Form and Antiform

This is the same lesson that the premier postmodern African American novel attempts to depict. Ishmael Reed's *Mumbo Jumbo*[46] shows these two opposing forces as they have occurred in African and African American history and culture. He juxtaposes the rigid Egyptian structuralism, with its emphasis on power and order, with the spontaneous character of West African–based religions. In this novel Reed describes the phenomenon of "Jes Grew."

"Jes Grew" is the spontaneous eruption of spirit that throws those whom it possesses into joyful fits of dance and shouts. It is opposed by those who trace their heritage through the Western trajectory of the religion of the powerful monotheistic Father God, who had its origin in ancient Egypt. "Jes Grew's" inheritors are best seen in the religion of Vodun, with its multiple gods who emphasize the presence of the divine spirit through possession.

Spontaneity and Improvisation

The urge toward respectability by the black middle class has made it difficult to maintain this humanizing postmodern nature of African American religion. There is nothing in the genes of Africans in America that can prevent blacks from imitating the religion of their conquerors. Wherever the spirit is, however, there is liberty, and this spirit of play and improvisation continues to find a home in the most unlikely places in the black community.

Reed correctly understands the ancient yet timeless nature of the stylistic combat between modernity and postmodernity. By tracing the development of the modernistic spirit to an ancient African culture, he deconstructs the racist argument that Africans have had little effect on the modern world. He also deconstructs the naive Afrocentric view that sees all things African, especially Egyptian, as worthy of praise and honor. Afrocentrists often give short shrift to the creative activity of Africans in captivity in the Americas and of Africans from less literate societies. The valorization of Egyptian culture runs the risk of naively accepting the despotic and rigid characteristics that also marked Egyptian dynastic society.

Reed's perceptive interpretation of the development of Western culture also indicts the modern religious curriculum, which gives little weight to the study of ancient African civilizations. African American theology and literary criticism have been handicapped because their critical methods emphasized the categories of modernity. I hope that it is

apparent why those categories, which were created by modern intellectuals, could not capture the essence of African cultural products, which
were postmodern in their very structure.

African American culture is deeply religious. African American religion reflects oral cultures that privilege discourses of the spirit. In this
discourse are spontaneity, improvisation, and great creativity. The logocentric discourses of modernity, which place an emphasis on static
descriptions of stable phenomena, have little chance of capturing the
essence of African American religion and culture.

Black Literary Criticism and Narrative Hermeneutics

Black Literary Criticism and Black Culture: The Black Aesthetic Movement of the 1960s

Contemporary black literary critics, like black theologians, have also been concerned with developing an adequate methodology for interpreting African American narratives. Like their counterparts in religious studies, which we examined in chapter 1, literary critics are also interested in developing a narrative hermeneutic that provides an interpretive framework for African American culture.

The historical forces that stirred the development of black theology—namely, the civil rights and black power movements—also were at work in the development of black literary criticism. Black literary critics have attempted to develop a view of black culture and language that satisfies the need to demonstrate the unique features of black literature and culture while developing an appropriate political stance for an oppressed people. This task is complicated by literary critics who also are concerned with maintaining or gaining status for black studies in the Western academic community.

Black literary critics have moved from the black aesthetic movement of the 1960s to the development of "high cultural" theories that would be acceptable for teaching in institutions of higher learning. The work of two of the leaders of the black criticism movement, Houston A. Baker Jr. and Henry Louis Gates Jr., demonstrates the methodological and constructive shifts in this burgeoning field.

Black literary critics have had greater success in gaining recognition for their ideas in the academy than have black theologians. This success may be due to their use of accepted academic critical theories and to their close attention to black narrative sources. However, just as with their black theological counterparts, their overreliance on methodologies that do not consistently reflect the cultural structures of the African American community unintentionally subverts their stated purpose of developing an African American narrative hermeneutic.

The latent possibilities for developing a cultural-structural African American hermeneutic are demonstrated most clearly in the writings of the founders of the black aesthetic movement. Larry Neal, an early spokesperson, says:

> The Black Arts Movement is radically opposed to any concept of the artist that alienates him from his community. Black Art is the aesthetic and spiritual sister of the Black Power concept. As such, it envisions an art that speaks directly to the needs and aspirations of Black America. In order to perform this task, The Black Arts Movement proposes a radical reordering of the Western cultural aesthetic. It proposes a separate symbolism, mythology, critique, and iconology. The Black Arts and the Black Power concept both relate broadly to the African American's desire for self-determination and nationhood. Both concepts are nationalistic. One is concerned with the relationship between art and politics; the other with the art of politics.[1]

The work of Stephen Henderson, another founder of this movement, was particularly important in developing hermeneutical categories for the criticism of African American poetic works. He attempted to develop a theory that was true to the black aesthetic.[2] In *Understanding the New Black Poetry*, Henderson attempts to identify the stylistic features of black narratives. He lists five criteria for determining whether a work of poetry should be included as an African American work of art[3]:

1. Any poetry from persons of black African ancestry can be placed in the category of African American narration.
2. The poetry must be structurally black, regardless of who the author may be. This means that both black and nonblack authors can pro-

duce black art. However, black authors who do not write in structurally black styles may not, indeed, be "black" writers.

3. Poetry by a person or group that is structurally, thematically, or otherwise characteristic of black African ancestry by persons or groups of
black African ancestry.

4. Poetry is judged to be poetry by black people when it is created by
identifiably black people. The ultimate criterion of whether an artist
is to be judged an African American artist is placed in the province
of the African American community. It also allows for the creation
of new styles that may be incorporated by the African American community.

5. Poetry whose ideological stance is judged to be correct vis-à-vis the
history and aspirations of blacks as judged by blacks.

Henderson insisted that these criteria suggest the kinds of issues that
need to be addressed in the identification of poetic black cultural works.
He did not address them thoroughly in this work, but he suggested that
these criteria would be essential elements in the development of black
literary theory. He hoped that these criteria would serve to stimulate
further discussion.

I think the early proponents of black literary criticism, including the
likes of radical artist and community activist LeRoi Jones (later, Amiri
Baraka), would insist that the critical endeavor involves both the cultural
and political aspirations of the black community. Henderson's schema
obviously emphasizes the political nature of this task without losing sight
of the essential features of black narration. His emphasis on what I have
termed a cultural-structural methodology is evident.

The black aesthetic movement went hand in hand with the black
power movement's quest for self-determination and political freedom.
This political aspect underlay blacks' need to determine criteria for the
canon of black works of art. The black theology movement also insisted
that black theology should be concerned with black liberation. However,
the nascent black theology movement did not ground its reflections in
the cultural structures of African American religious narration.

As a culturally political movement, the black aesthetic movement
sought to have the black voice determine the shape of the canon and
the rules for interpretation. This struggle for black power was waged at
the level of discourse, with a recognition that the power of interpretation
grounds the struggle for self-determination.

The first movement of criticism in Henderson's schema concerns the determination that the voice is an African American voice. This did not mean that nonblacks were excluded. If they fulfilled the cultural or political requirements of black writing, then they could be included in the sphere of black art. Henderson then suggests that the interpretive process proceed according to the requirements of three critical categories: theme, structure, and saturation.[4]

Theme

The critic of black art must be concerned with the identification and interpretation of particular themes present in black literature. According to Henderson, liberation is a key theme for genuine black work. Henderson includes the work songs, blues, jazz, spirituals, and sermons in his consideration of African American poetic narration. He states that the theme of liberation was an early feature of black poetry in America and that these sources of black poetry have the theme of liberation as a central and recurring motif.

Henderson believes that the liberation motif plays two important roles in black life and critical thought. On the one hand, the black community's expressions of liberation helped it survive in an oppressive culture. On the other hand, the critic must acknowledge the presence of liberation themes in art as liberation becomes a key to the hermeneutic process. The process of interpretation is concerned with liberation because the material under critique has a distinctively political message. This concern with the political nature of black narration is also seen in the development of black theological reflection by James Cone, author of the first black theology.

Structure

Henderson believes that the structural analysis is the most difficult aspect of black narration. He identifies several features of black poetic structure: virtuoso naming and enumerating, jazz rhythmic effect, virtuoso free rhyming, hyperbolic imagery, metaphysical imagery, understatement, compressed and cryptic imagery, and worrying the line.

In his discussion of the structural characteristics of African American narratives, Henderson writes about the relationship of structure to saturation:

> Perhaps the hallmark of successful use is wit, which listeners and readers instantly recognize and respond to in a manner similar to their response to metaphysical imagery, but in addition to the pleasure of intellectual surprise there is the added dimension of defying social taboo. Frankly, at times one arrives at a kind of rock-bottom truth which is memorably expressed. . . . For example, Imamu Baraka's (LeRoi Jones) "Pretty-ditty" hinges on the last line and especially on the hyperbolic but subtle in-group meanings of "motherfucker." Although Don Lee's "The Wall" hinges on the same word, also in a hyperbolic sense, the meaning suggests appreciative awe and scales off into personally and communally recognized meanings which are more felt than named, in other words, into a condition of "saturation."[5]

It should be noted that the black aesthetic movement, like much of black political thought in the 1960s, was plagued with sexist assumptions in its political thought, literary canons, and, as in this example, its choice of images. I hope that my insistence on "rapetalistic oppression" as the predominant social paradigm for understanding the creation of black narration will address the need to take into account the gendered experiences of black females and males in the critical process.

Saturation

Henderson defines *saturation* as the communication of blackness in a given situation and a sense of fidelity to the observed and intuited truth of the black experience. This category has more to do with the community's or critic's recognition that the work of art is reminiscent of the black experience and ethos than with a tangible, easily explained cultural structure.

Saturation covers a sense of feeling and political awareness. It is a difficult category for the critic to explicate because of its aesthetic or feeling-based sensibility. We also saw the importance of feeling in the discussion of African American religion. Henderson views saturation as similar to the term *soul* as it was used to increase group solidarity during the time of black awareness and protest.

Religion and Black Literary Criticism

It is apparent that Henderson's stylistic categories—theme, structure, and saturation—still hold interpretive power for the development of an African American narrative hermeneutic. These categories allow the critic to develop a systematic and complex structural analysis of black narrative style. This mode of analysis, coupled with a metaphoric analysis, is capable of identifying and analyzing the major cultural-structural features in African American religion and culture.

Henderson's identification of liberation as a major theme does not mean that he sees this theme working solely or in isolation in African American literature. He illustrates this point through use of the spirituals:

> In the oral tradition, the dogged determination of the work songs, the tough-minded power of the blues, the inventive energy of jazz, and the transcendent vision of God in the spirituals and the sermons, all energize the idea of Liberation, which is itself liberated from the temporal, the societal, and the political—not with the narcotic obsession to remain above the world of struggle and change and death, but with full realization of a return to that world both strengthened and renewed. Thus in the spirituals we have both.[6]

In this passage, Henderson reveals his understanding of the complexity of African American thought, especially as it involves the religious world of African Americans, in which liberation themes and more conventional themes of transcendence exist in creative interplay.

Contemporary Black Literary Criticism: Vernacular Theory

Blues Vernacular Theory

To explore the difficulties in the development of a black narrative theory, we will examine two leading figures in the development of contemporary black literary theory. Houston Baker Jr. has had a significant impact on the field of black literary criticism. In *The Journey Back*, Baker states that black critics must be engaged in the "anthropology of art." This book is Baker's attempt to develop a thorough exploration of methodology in black literary criticism in light of African American history and culture.[7] Baker's methodology here is consistent with the terms of Henderson's initial effort. Baker insists that black criticism must engage in what cultural anthropologist Clifford Geertz terms "thick description." Black criticism must be an interdisciplinary process by which cultural practices and ideas are analyzed by describing and attempting to retrieve the meanings of a culture as seen within that culture's system of meaning. Baker is confident that the resources of cultural and symbolic anthropology will be valuable methodological partners in this attempt.[8]

Baker is critical of scholars who attempt to interpret the meaning and significance of black cultural works outside the context of that society's cultural perspective. He believes that this runs the risk of faulty interpretation of African and African American culture, and he offers the work of Larry Neal as an illustration.

> Let us take, for example, the disorientation one experiences when one sees a piece of African sculpture in a Madison Avenue art gallery. Ask yourself: What is it doing there? In Africa, the piece had ritual significance. It was a spiritual affirmation of the connection between man and his ancestors, and it implied a particular kind of ontology—a particular sense of being. . . . In the gallery or the salon it is merely an objet d'art, but for your [black American] ancestors, it was a bridge between them and the spirit, a bridge between you and your soul in the progression of a spiritual lineage.[9]

Baker's early work, like Neal's and Henderson's, insisted on the political nature of black criticism and emphasized the need to develop appropriate cultural-structural tools for the interpretation of black narration and culture.

Only at Baker's most thorough work, *Blues, Ideology and Afro-American Literature: A Vernacular Theory,* does he make a fateful turn in the development of his black literary theory. Here he attempts to develop what he terms a "vernacular" theory of black literary criticism.[10] Although Baker employs many methodological sources, his work could be defined as a combination of Hegelian, neo-Marxist, and postmodern strategies. When Baker actually interprets black slave narratives, which he calls the "locus classicus" of black literature, he develops a materialist critique in which he employs the categories of "economics of slavery" and "commercial deportation" as key hermeneutic categories. Baker asserts that the slave narratives and other black works of art are primarily concerned with African Americans' abilities to negotiate their economic independence.[11]

Baker employs the term *blues* as a metaphor for the black condition in particular and for the American situation in general. The social contexts in which blacks found themselves were marked by a blues energy and perspective. He relies on postmodern insights to insist that this blues matrix was the subtext at work in the production of American culture. In effect, this matrix "spoke" through black and other American works of art. African Americans did not simply create the blues; the blues created black and American culture as well: "In my book *The Journey Back: Issues in Black Literature and Criticism* (1980), I envisioned the 'speaking subject' creating language (a code) to be deciphered by the present-day commentator. In my current study, I envision language (the code) 'speaking' the subject. The subject is 'decentered.' "[12] Baker's analysis depends on deconstructionist notions of the "always already" nature of the social context in which persons and societies are influenced by a matrix of effects in their social and linguistic world."[13]

Baker privileges the structure of Eurocentric analyses. Therefore, he cannot come to terms with the religious nature of the generating black code, because he proposes a methodology that is not faithful to the black cultural experience. By contrast, DuBois and Hurston identified the importance of religion in the lives of the African American community while not demeaning or ignoring the religious basis of African American culture.

In an article about his poststructuralist methodology, Baker explains his movement away from his earlier structuralist position. He speaks of the development of his new theoretical position which no longer privileges structuralist discourse:

> The metaphors likely to prevail in a universe of Afro-American literary-theoretical discourse are metaphors drawn from the "vernacular." By the vernacular I want to suggest not only the majority of Afro-American, but, in both an economic and a political sense, the American majority. . . . My own first model for arriving at adequate answers to such questions was drawn from the realm of symbolic anthropology. I believed that an interdisciplinary account predicated on the assumption of "Man as Speaking Subject" and employing resources of contemporary linguistic

theory would illuminate the way in which Afro-American literary works of art functioned as uniquely expressive behavior that received the positive judgement of the Afro-American community. In more recent work, my metaphorical grounding has shifted from man as speaker to the text conceived of as an always/already spoken.[14]

This represents a definitive shift from an interpretation that privileges description of African American culture to a methodology that utilizes the language and concepts of academic discourse. Although this enterprise is appropriate for a scholar, it makes it more difficult to maintain the trajectory of the black aesthetic movement, whose members primarily were concerned with delineating and expressing themselves in the black idiom.

Baker attributes this shift in theory to his encounter with the dialectical thought of Frederick Jameson, Hayden White, Marshall Sahlins, and Hegel. This methodology moves from a centered to a decentered subject, in which Baker privileges the social background rather than the foreground of African American discourse.[15]

Baker makes this move too hastily. For instance, his work tends to obscure the black tradition by ignoring its religious foundations, a position one does not find in Henderson's work. Instead, what is needed is a clearly delineated picture of the African American tradition in which religion is not treated as an epiphenomenon of social and economic factors. The African American tradition suffers from a lack of knowledge of the centered or "speaking subject." The full delineation of the African American tradition has been hindered by a cultural conspiracy that has denigrated all things African and African American. This functioning of racist power has limited our understanding of African American knowledge. Baker is aware that this methodology diverges from his earlier, more culturally sensitive perspective. However, he is convinced that this move is necessary for his continued interpretation of African American culture.[16]

Baker cannot have his cake and eat it, too. However true he intends to be to the use of black categories, Baker allows for the possibility of deviation from the goals of the black aesthetic movement when he depends too heavily on methodologies that move away from black cultural categories. Because those disciplines have been the province of Western European thought, Baker must be extremely careful that other modes of analyzing discourse do not supersede the African American cultural voice. To avoid this, he must clearly establish the relationship of the use of interdisciplinary methods to the norms of black culture.

This task is crucial, for it will determine how capable his method is of interpreting black works of art as they are understood by the African American community. Henderson accomplishes this task by emphasizing its descriptive nature and by allowing the texts to suggest their own norms and patterns. The methods of social scientists whose intent is to allow the culture under study to suggest its own categories of expression could, as Baker suggests, be an important tool for this project. However, he makes little or no use of black metaphoric themes, and does not allow his narrators to define their own cultural categories.

Baker's reliance on a blues matrix does not cohere with the black community's understanding of the blues; instead, the blues matrix becomes a catchall for the generation of sacred and secular cultural forms, not to mention a multitude of black narrative forms:

> The blues are synthesis (albeit one always synthesizing rather than one already hypostatized). Combining work songs, group seculars, field hollers, sacred harmonies, proverbial wisdom, folk philosophy, political commentary, ribald humor, elegiac lament, and much more, they constitute an amalgam that seems always to have been in motion in America— always becoming, shaping, transforming, displacing the peculiar experiences of Africans in the New World.[17]

One difficulty with Baker's reliance on the blues as the primary code for black expression is that this is an ahistorical perspective. Henderson correctly recognized the place and priority of religious themes, especially the spirituals, as the historical root of African American existence and cultural life. Although Baker is aware of this religious foundation of African American and American society, nevertheless, he collapses the "sacred harmonies" into this blues category.

The critic would better serve the African American community by deconstructing forms of knowledge that have hidden these cultural meanings, even from those who practice them. This is not meant to denigrate Marxist and neo-Marxist forms of analysis. They may, in fact, aid in this dialectical process of cultural recovery as they demonstrate how the economic motives of the dominant culture have aided in this racist practice of denial and denigration of black culture. The African

American community has a long history of participation in the Marxist dialogue, but this participation should not come at the expense of African American culture.[18]

I find myself more in agreement with Henderson and with Baker's earlier attempts to develop a structuralist interdisciplinary methodology. This methodology attempts to employ a cultural-structural hermeneutic of African American narratives, a structuralism that is concerned with a "thick description" of the narratives of African American religion and culture.

Baker's argument for his methodological shift is unconvincing. Even though Baker's work represents a sincere desire to use the latest critical theories on African American discourse, he does not provide convincing reasons why this methodological shift is necessary. It is one thing to be impressed by the deserved impact of the latest dialectical theories of critical theorists, but it is another thing to provide a coherent and consistent argument that their theories are necessary and important for the study of African American culture. Because Baker does not provide a rationale grounded in the black experience, the critic runs the risk of using methods that may be alien to the intentions of black popular culture.

Cultural and symbolic anthropologists at least have demonstrated an awareness of the difficulty in interpreting non-Western cultures because of the different orientations of those cultures. Baker allows the new "interdisciplinary" orientation of his work to overwhelm the African American voice. His earnest desire is to develop a method of criticism that is true to black culture, but it is doubtful if Henderson or Neal would validate this attempt at developing a black literary theory that seems to undermine the unique qualities of black art. Even the use of blues, an indigenous category, does not serve as the main interpretive principle.

Craig Werner, in his discussion of the work of other black literary critics, shares a similar view:

> In fact, critics such as Henry Louis Gates, Jr. . . . and Robert Stepto . . . have demonstrated the real potential for the application of aspects of contemporary theory to the criticism of Afro-American literature. Nonetheless, the pressure to "authenticate" (to use Stepto's term) all critical positions by employing the language of avant-garde discourse strikes me as a manifestation of . . . "cultural solipsism." It seems to me particularly

important that critics involved with Afro-American literature resist this
pressure or risk contributing to the effective silencing of their own
voices.[19]

In order to demonstrate this "cultural solipsism," one need only examine Baker's definition of the blues, his key critical metaphor. In
Baker's hands this definition is so broad as to lose any sense of the
lived experience of the African American community. Baker not only
has combined almost every possible aspect of African American culture
under the blues rubric but also denies African Americans' ownership of
their own narrative productions. In Baker's account, the African American community did not create the blues and other narrative products;
instead, they were produced by the script they encountered in the New
World. The religious voice is also subsumed under the secular formation of the blues, something that is not reflected in black cultural
awareness.[20]

Baker's interpretation, unlike the cultural anthropological structuralism of Geertz, renders African American culture as subjectless and
ahistorical. This theoretical stance does not do justice to the creative
genius of African Americans who produced these blues narratives in the
social context of extreme suffering with only their cultural sensibility to
aid them in their struggle to maintain their humanity, humor, and
convictions. Baker places too much emphasis on the context without
drawing interpretive attention to the complex cultural reality of those
who responded to the context with a particular narrative art form. The
blues are a decidedly secular response, with some overtly religious overtones, to the oppressive situation of blacks. The difference between the
production of secular and sacred musical narratives can be seen by examining the historical development of black culture. Gospel music, for
instance, was a religious discourse that took its musical form from the
blues. It combined a blues form with themes from the spirituals to
produce a form of narration that appealed to the contemporary black
consciousness.

Secular and sacred forms can be combined and mixed in black culture, but the black community itself understands that there are differences between the blues and religious forms of musical narration. The
structural features we discussed are present in both cases, but differences
in thematic content distinguish them. Baker's attempt to subsume re-

ligious music under his blues rubric does violence to the black community's history and self-understanding. It also reveals Baker's difficulty in accepting the religious dimension of African American culture.

Religion and Blues Vernacular Theory: Slave Narratives

It is unfortunate that the religious voice of African Americans has become problematic for many post-1960s black intellectuals. In Baker's examination of selected slave narratives we see that black religion is problematic for him. In fact, Baker asserts that centering the critical interpretation around the religious statements of black subjects is a mistake. In a one-sided Marxist interpretation, he treats black religiosity like an illusion that hides the real economic activity of black subjects.

Baker interprets the slave narratives of Frederick Douglass and Olaudah Equiano (Gustavus Vassa) to buttress his claims that their voices are primarily those of economics. Baker claims that the religious voice decreases as the economic voice increases.[21] He sees these two elements in tension; in fact, they coexist as mutual partners in the text. It does not take a particularly exhaustive reading to determine that the religious voice actually increases in the narratives of Equiano and Douglass as they develop their individual economic capacities. In the passage Baker cites to attempt to prove this diminution of the black religious voice, he conveniently overlooks the presence of the religious voice in which Equiano also praises God for his new found freedom:[22]

> My master then said, he would not be worse than his promise; and, taking the money, told me to go to the Secretary of the Register Office, and get my manumission drawn up.
>
> These words of my master were like a voice from heaven to me: in an instant all my trepidation was turned into unutterable bliss; and I most reverently bowed myself with gratitude, unable to express my feeling, but by the overflowing of my eyes, and a heart replete with thanks to God; while my true and worthy friend, the Captain, congratulated us both with a peculiar degree of heartfelt pleasure. As soon as the first transports of my joy were over, and that I had expressed my thanks to these my worthy friends in the best manner I was able, I rose with a heart full of affection and reverence, and left the room, in order to obey my master's joyful mandate of going to the Register Office. As I was leaving the house I called to mind the words of the Psalmist, in the 126th

Psalm, and like him, "I glorified God in my heart, in whom I trusted."
These words had been impressed on my mind from the very day I was
forced from Deptford on the present hour, and I now saw them, as I
thought, fulfilled and verified.[23]

Instead of acknowledging the coexistence of an African American
religious voice, Baker interprets Equiano's account from a Eurocentric
religious perspective. He rightly is concerned that Equiano's narrative
not be read as simply an example of a Christian tract, but he seemingly
is unaware of a distinctive African American religious voice that accepted
the discourse of evangelical Christianity while using it for its own eman-
cipatory purposes. This is as true of the slave narratives as it was of the
spirituals. Acknowledging this, however, requires a subject that speaks
and creates a tradition as well as one that is affected by language and
social conditions.[24]

Baker assumes that the only alternative religious reading of this text
is one derived from a Eurocentric Christian perspective. This assumption allows him to propose an alternative economic reading of the text
that obscures the possibility of an African American religious-cultural
reading, a reading that would allow the complex interplay of Equiano's
religious and economic voices to stand. Baker is unaware of an African
American religious ethic that validated certain evangelical Christian ideas
while also validating the African cultural and religious heritage. But this
ethic is seen clearly in Equiano's remarkable depiction of his African
religious background:

> As to religion, the natives believe that there is one Creator of all things,
> and that he lives in the sun, and is girted round with a belt; that he may
> never eat or drink, but, according to some, he smokes a pipe, which is
> our own favorite luxury. They believe he governs events, especially our
> deaths or captivity; but, as for the doctrine of eternity, I do not remember
> to have ever heard of it; some, however, believe in the transmigration of
> souls in a certain degree. Those spirits which were relations, they believe
> always attend them, and guard them from the bad spirits or their foes.
> For this reason not transmigrated, such as their dear friends or they
> always, before eating, as I have observed, eat some small portion of the
> meat, and pour some of their drink, on the ground for them; and they
> often make oblations of the blood of beasts or fowls at their graves. I
> was very fond of my mother, and almost constantly with her. When she
> went to make these oblations at her mother's tomb, which was a kind

of small solitary thatched house, I sometimes attended her. There she made her libations, and spent most of the night in cries and lamentations. . . . We practiced circumcision like the Jews, and made offerings and feasts on that occasion, in the same manner as they did. Like them also, our children were named from some event, some circumstance, or fancied foreboding at the time of their birth. I was named "Olaudah," which in our language signifies vicissitude, or fortunate. . . . I remember we never polluted the name of the object of our adoration; on the contrary, it was always mentioned with the greatest reverence.[25]

Instead of centering on Equiano's supposed Eurocentric theology and ethics, Baker could have examined the complete religious context from which Equiano writes as proof of an African American strategy that encompasses and uses both the European and African religious contexts. Because Equiano and his African compatriots are constrained by the prevailing notions of African religious inferiority, they must, in effect, create a new form of Christianity that is truly dialectical in its attention to their historical tradition and their encounter with modernity. This new religious form supersedes the knowledge or expectations of the European community that they are addressing. Unfortunately, African Americans' ability to maintain this dialectical theology waned as American blacks became convinced of the inferiority of African-based religious practices and beliefs.[26]

We must remember that Equiano is writing within a social world that has accepted traditional Christian notions of the providence and sovereignty of God. For Equiano to write in another way would have compromised his credibility and limited his listeners' ability to aid him and his kinsmen in their cause. Yet he was able to convey his positive regard for the religion and culture of his West African homeland.

A further reading of the text reveals that the religious dimension lies at the center of Equiano's interpretation of his life and freedom. It is a religious vision that conforms, at least in its doctrinal statements, to traditional Christian notions, but it also affirms conceptions of human freedom and dignity. Equiano's rhetoric is reminiscent of African American notions of signifying (i.e., the use of a double voice through ironic rhetoric). Equiano "signifies" or criticizes his readers concerning their presuppositions about the integrity of the African religious and cultural task in a way that also leaves him free to appeal to their Christian sensibilities for the support of African liberation.[27]

Baker allows his materialist and deconstructionist perspective to over-whelm what actually is occurring culturally and historically in the black texts. This also is true of his analysis of the *Narrative of Frederick Douglass*, where he argues, as he did for Equiano, that the economic voice is the privileged voice.[28]

Baker determines that revolt and literacy, like religion, also are in-capable of achieving black freedom. These passages reveal the ways in which Baker allows his wedding to Marxist and deconstructionist thought to distort the meanings of the African American narrative voice.[29] Baker must be aware of the thin line he is treading, for after this cited passage he writes:

> What one experiences in the conclusions of Equiano's and Douglass's narratives, however, is identity with a difference. For the expressive, married, economically astute self at the close of Douglass's work represents a convergence of the voices that mark the various autobiographical postures of the *Narrative* as a whole. The orator whom we see standing at a Nantucket convention at the close of Douglass's work is immediately to become a "salaried" spokesman, combining literacy, Christianity, and revolutionary zeal in an individual and economically profitable job of work. Douglass's authorship, oratory, and economics converge in the history of the *Narrative*'s publication and the course of action its appearance mandated in the life of the author.[30]

This is the position from which Baker should have begun his analysis. Instead of attempting to privilege the economic voice, as his theory calls for, a close reading of the text reveals that religious, economic, and other voices are in full play.[31]

In a careful and thoroughly thick descriptive reading of the narratives, one readily can see this combination of means for achieving freedom. One might wonder whether Baker is defending the right of today's "black man of talent who would be free" to gain as much individual wealth as possible in order to buy his freedom, for this privileging of the economic voice certainly was not the only consideration or the common attitude among black slaves toward buying one's freedom.

Baker omits the sense of tragedy and outrage that also accompanied this purchase of freedom. In the slave narrative of Linda Brent, we get another view of the "economics of slavery." Of an exchange between her former master and friend, she writes:

"I mean Linda, that ran away from Dr. Flint's plantation, some years ago. I dare say you've seen her, and know where she is."

"Yes, sir, I've seen her, and know where she is. She is out of your reach, sir."

"Tell me where she is, or bring her to me, and I will give her a chance to buy her freedom."

"I don't think it would be of any use, sir. I have heard her say she would go to the ends of the earth, rather than pay any man or woman for her freedom, because she thinks she has a right to it. Besides, she couldn't do it, if she would, for she has spent her earnings to educate her children."[32]

Brent continues the narrative:

In a few days one came from Mrs. Bruce, informing me that my new master was still searching for me, and that she intended to put an end to this persecution by buying my freedom. I felt grateful for the kindness that prompted this offer, but the idea was not so pleasant to me as might have been expected. The more my mind had become enlightened, the more difficult it was for me to consider myself an article of property; and to pay money to those who had so grievously oppressed me seemed like taking from my sufferings the glory of triumph.[33]

After Brent's freedom is purchased, she writes these lines:

My brain reeled as I read these lines. A gentleman near me said, "It's true; I have seen the bill of sale." "The bill of sale!" Those words struck me like a blow. So I was "sold" at last! A human being "sold" in the free city of New York! The bill of sale is on record, and future generations will learn from it that women were articles of traffic in New York, late in the nineteenth century of the Christian religion. It may hereafter prove a useful document to antiquaries, who are seeking to measure the progress of civilization in the United States. I well know the value of that bit of paper; but much as I love freedom, I do not like to look upon it. I am deeply grateful to the generous friend who procured it, but I despise the miscreant who demanded payment for what never rightfully belonged to him or his.[34]

Brent expresses joy and relief over the end of her ordeal, but she does not believe, as does Baker, that freedom is simply a matter of economics. The numerous incidents of slave runaways and revolts also should be a convincing argument against the idea that nineteenth-century blacks simply saw their freedom in economic terms. The religious and moral voice almost always accompanies the economic voice in slave narratives. In fact, Douglass's inclusion of a theological interpretation of American Christianity in the epilogue of his narrative is proof par excellence of the privileging, or at least of the coexistence and weaving, of the religious voice in the narratives of African Americans.[35]

Baker's economic reading of the African American captive's voice is also extended to his analysis of the role of gender in Brent's narrative:

> With the foregoing analysis in mind, it is possible to assert that gender does not alter a fundamentally commercial set of negotiations represented as liberating in the black narrative. The gender of Brent and her narrator does, however, immeasurably broaden the descriptive scope of "commercial deportation" and the "economics of slavery." The implied domain of sexual victimization so briefly represented in male narratives becomes the dramatically foregrounded "topos" of the woman's account. And the subtextual dimensions of Afro-American narrative that receive full voice "only" in the work of the black woman include representations of the psychologically perverse motivations of the patriarch-as-rapist, the female slave's manipulation of a sexual and financial partnership outside the boundaries of the master's power, and the strategy of retreat that leads to commercial advantage and physical freedom.[36]

In fairness to Baker, he does allow that Brent's status as a woman lends a sense of community to her narrative that is missing from male slave narratives. Baker may be correct in maintaining that women have more communal sense when they write, but his analysis of Brent's narrative is so thin that this interpretation seems to be little more than an afterthought or a bow to current feminist critical theories.[37]

Baker has allowed his embrace of interdisciplinary modes of thought to obscure other modes of thought, which, in turn, distorts the lived reality of his African American subjects. Even his use of the blues as a metaphor for his black vernacular theory turns out to be a category that has more meaning for America than it has for an illumination of the black experience.

Baker is not doing "anthropology of art" based on thick description of black narratives and social context. Instead, he is analyzing black culture with Eurocentric academic methodological tools that have limited disclosive power for analyzing African American narratives in their cultural complexity. This amounts to the kind of cultural imperialism that Henderson, Neal, Cone, and Long have been attempting to avoid.

To be effective, Baker would need to thoroughly delineate the blues structure of African American culture in some of the ways that Henderson suggests. Baker is well aware of Henderson's work and places himself within the same black aesthetic stream. However, he gives no credible reason for abandoning Henderson's position.[38]

Baker is closer to developing an adequate African American narrative hermeneutic in his earlier work, *The Journey Back*. Here he shows more sensitivity to the role that African culture and religion play in the work of Equiano. In this work, Baker reflects his understanding of the dialectical process that Equiano underwent in his journey from Africa to becoming a founder of the African American literary tradition.[39] This involves, as we saw, the presence of religious ideology, African understandings of culture and freedom, and the African American struggle for liberation. Baker also reveals the same understanding of Frederick Douglass's narrative.[40]

Even so, it is unfortunate that Baker is not more familiar with the work of the historians of African American religion that we examined in chapter 2. If so, he probably would have been more hesitant to blithely label Douglass's rhetoric as simply reflective of the white Christian abolitionist perspective. His use of the blues as a metaphor for his critique is a hopeful sign that he still is in contact with particular black modes of structuring reality. Yet, he never adequately defines the blues from a black viewpoint. Baker's use of the blues as an all-inclusive metaphor is simply inadequate for an examination of American and African American literature and culture. The religious voice has been a significant—if not the most prominent—response of European and African Americans in the New World to the prospects of tyranny and slavery. Baker's analysis distorts this role for the sake of developing the blues as the operative metaphor of black cultural criticism from a Eurocentric perspective.

Black Literary Theory

Signifyin' Henry Louis Gates Jr., a contemporary of Baker in black literary circles, has also attempted to develop a hermeneutic of African

American literature that is true to academic and African American modes of discourse. Baker's development of a literary theory in *Blues* is in dialogue with Gates's ideas: in fact, Baker claims a kind of methodological victory by stating that Gates now has adopted his terminology of "vernacular" for black cultural criticism.[41]

Gates has left his own mark in black literary circles. A winner of the prestigious MacArthur Fellowship, Gates has written several influential articles and books about black literary criticism. The most cogent statements of his theoretical position are found in " 'Race,' Writing and Difference," in articles in *Black Literature and Literary Theory,* and in two books, *Figures in Black: Words, Signs and the "Racial" Self* and *The Signifying Monkey: A Theory of Afro-American Literary Criticism.*[42]

Gates and Baker claim to have serious differences, yet they agree on some important things. Both are committed to demonstrating how a mastery of the discourse of scholarly critical theories can illumine the interpretation of black works of art. Both also are committed to developing a literary discourse that does justice to the style of African American narrative.

Unlike Baker, Gates has explored the African foundations of black literature by tracing it to forms found in West African traditional religion in general and the religion of the Yoruba in particular. In *The Signifying Monkey,* the book most representative of his literary theory, he delves into the significance of West African religious mythology and cosmology to develop an appropriate basis for criticism. However, he makes much less extensive use of African American religion in his analyses. In ways like Baker's, Gates makes liberal use of poststructural scholarship in semiotics and tropic analysis. This goal is central to Gates's project; at the same time, he wishes to keep black theories of cultural criticism in the forefront:

> I once thought it our most important gesture to *master* the canon of criticism, to *imitate* and *apply* it, but I now believe that we must turn to the black tradition itself to develop theories of criticism indigenous to our literatures. . . .
>
> To attempt to appropriate our own discourses by using Western critical theory uncritically is to substitute one mode of neocolonialism for another. To begin to do that in my own tradition, theorists have turned to the black vernacular tradition—to paraphrase Jackson, they have begun to dig into the depths of the tradition of our foreparents—to isolate

the signifying black difference through which to theorize about the so-called discourse of the Other.[43]

Gates also uses the work of Geneva Smitherman, a black sociolinguist of African American language, in developing his theory of black signification. Unlike Smitherman, however, Gates attempts to formulate black literary criticism in Western academic terms. While attempting to develop a black literary theory that is free of Western critical domination, he uses the black linguistic category of "signifyin' " as a particularly important means of understanding black narratives. In his early attempts at explaining "signifyin'," Gates attempts to equate this black term with the academic critical concept of signification, and he attempts to locate it historically from its West African and African American usage.[44]

This equation of *signifyin'* and *signification* is a tenuous connection. Gates seems to be guilty of justifying black language usage by comparing it to Western academic terms, which in his own language is a form of neocolonialism in an academic context. Baker had this same tendency toward cultural solipsism, in which black theorists seek to justify their theoretical positions by reference to Western academic categories of interpretation. If Gates simply took the black language usage of signifying to interpret his texts, then he would not be guilty of a neocolonial form of literary criticism. However, this necessity to constantly equate and compare African and African American linguistic structures with European features diminishes an otherwise significant insight into the way that black cultural categories can be used to provide hermeneutic norms.

African Religion and Black Literary Theory Gates enlarges this black cultural linguistic feature of signification in *The Signifying Monkey* with an extensive treatment of the Yoruba trickster god Esu-Elegbara as the "author" of signifying in the West African and African American culture.[45] Gates claims that African Americans appropriated a concept they had received from their West African ancestors and used it as a guide for a conceptual schema for structuring their own narration. Therefore, black language is best interpreted as a process of signifying, as this process becomes the "master trope" of African American narration. This trope subsumes under it other tropes of metaphor, metonym, synecdoche, irony, aporia, chiasmus, and catachresis.[46]

This trope is embodied in the African American trickster tales of the "signifyin' monkey," in which a monkey constantly outwits a much stronger animal, generally a lion. Gates understands that this signifying monkey figure is analogous to the Yoruban trickster god, Esu: "If Esu stands for discourse upon a text, then his Pan-African kinsman, the Signifying Monkey, stands for the rhetorical strategies of which each literary text consist. For the Signifying Monkey exists as the great trope of Afro-American discourse, and the trope of tropes, his language of Signifyin(g), is his verbal sign in the Afro-American tradition."[47]

Gates states that this trope is inherently related to reversal. He identifies four modes of signifying in black texts; tropological revision, the speakerly text, talking texts, and Rewriting the Speakerly.[48] In developing these categories through a close reading of African American texts, Gates claims that black authors are in a signifying relationship with each other in that they have been and are continually referring to each others' texts and are in fact "signifying" with one another.

Unfortunately, Gates does not acknowledge that the West African pantheon is larger than the Yoruban trickster god, Esu. There also are gods of thunder, war, fertility, and the sea and rivers. Gates's fascination with showing how African American discourse "signifies" leads him to truncate the African religious experience. This truncation and Gates's method of comparing black to European cultural categories is problematic but not necessarily fatal for the development of a cultural hermeneutic west African is true to African and African American cultural discourse.[49]

Critical Dualism: Culture or Liberation

Earlier in his career, Gates rejected Henderson's attempts at developing criteria for a black aesthetic that included the categories of social and political protest on the grounds that it was too narrow in its cultural and political dimensions. He asserted that Henderson did not understand the universal characteristics of language in which black narratives also participate. In reality, Gates has not changed his position, although he now adds black cultural categories to his interpretive proces. This procedure, which seeks to separate the political from modes of universal cultural discourse, is at the root of Gates's reliance on Western forms of academic interpretation.[50]

My position is that all universal categories have specific cultural referents and expressions. Gates faults Henderson for identifying the aesthetic with the ethical. He asserts that a literary theory applied to black texts must be developed that demonstrates the complexity of black life and is not limited to themes of liberation and political action. Here Gates posits that the criticism of the Marxist literary critic Raymond Williams may be more helpful to black critics than the development of a black criticism based on a distinctive black culture. Gates, however, does not seem to understand that the power of Williams's work is his linking of Marxist notions of political struggle with the cultural struggles of working-class people.

African American slaves did not simply continue a tradition. They transformed it to fit their own cultural and political situation. But as long as Gates is silent about the oppressive political situation that influences the narration of the African American community, he cannot reveal the full dimension of signification in black literature and thereby demonstrate how African Americans transformed their African cultural heritage in the dialectical crucible of American oppression.

Although Gates ignores the political dimensions of African American narration, Henderson, Neal, and Baker all were able to see how black narration is inherently connected to the black situation of oppression and the struggle for liberation. Gates is silent about the decided influence of the oppressive nature of black life in America as a dialectical process that also can affect the creation of black narration. Gates may fear that if he acknowledged the influence of oppression on African American narration, his decision to treat signification in the African and African American context as an unbroken tradition would be undermined.

The signifying monkey tales in the American context generally are regarded as models for how black slaves dealt with an oppressive situation. The slaves' use of stealth and trickery was a necessary consequence of the oppressive dialectical relationship between masters and slaves. The African Esu tradition, however, is concerned instead with the ways in which humans are tested by the gods than with relationships between people. The story of Job is a more appropriate parallel to the intention of these Esu tales, as Satan attempts to test the character of Job by afflicting him with trying circumstances. This may be why some Christian missionaries tended to identify trickster figures with Satan.

Gates, like Baker, has come to see the importance of religion in the interpretation of African American culture, but both have difficulty integrating a fully nuanced understanding of African and African American religion into their literary theory. Baker attempts to make the "blues" the dominant religious and cultural metaphor of the African American cultural experience, but he has little sense of the role African American religion plays in relationship to and apart from blues sensibilities. Gates, in attempting to ground his critique in West African religion, recognizes the importance of religion, but he, too, fails to understand the vital role of the African American religious tradition in the development of the narrative process in African American cultural life.

This does not mean that Gates is totally oblivious to the role of African American religion in the development of black narration. In one essay, he recognizes the importance of African American spirituals to the development of black narrative works:

> Go down, Moses,
> Way down in Egypt land,
>   Tell ole Pharaoh,
> To let my people go.

> The stanza itself became, as we shall see, a reference point for much of black poetry, as did nearly all of the spirituals. The spirituals are of such import to black poetic language that when they surface as referents in the poetry—spoken, sung, or danced speech—they cannot but bear the full emotional and structural import of another lurking but not lost hermetic universe. Scores of reviews compared Paul Laurence Dunbar's "lyric" with songs (as did Dunbar). Spirituals as referents give black poetry an opulence of meaning—one translated through time and space by an oral tradition of over three and a half centuries not readily available to exterior exploration.[51]

It is unfortunate that Gates did not extend his understanding of the spirituals as the genesis of African American poetry to other works of black narration:

> It is right that the spirituals should be our reference point for dialect poetry, since the spirituals—"as anonymous as earth"—succeeded so well exactly where dialect was to fail: in using a new form to convey a new

meaning, a meaning inseparable from belief, both of which gave rise to that form. The lines from this standard European hymn, for example—

At this table we'll sit down.

Christ will gird himself and serve us sweet manna all round

—were translated into the lines

Gwine to sit down at the welcome table,
Gwine to feast off milk and honey.[52]

Gates demonstrates an awareness of how structure and meaning are related at the grammatical and phonetic level, but, by failing to understand how the spirituals as a new genre also are signifying the deepest meanings of the African American community, Gates displays the same ignorance of the African American religious tradition as did Baker. Gates and Baker also overlook the distinctive religious view held by African Americans in the slave narratives. Gates's expositions of the poetry of Phyllis Wheatley and the narrative of Frederick Douglass have almost no mention of their theological positions or religious experiences.[53]

It is ironic that Henderson and Neal, who were more radical politically, also were more aware of the contribution of African American religion to the creation of the foundational meanings of African American culture. Gates's attempt to skip over several hundred years of African American religious creativity by drawing on Yoruban systems of meaning and Baker's attempts to develop the blues into the dominant form by ignoring the significance of African American religion effectively rob those "nameless bards"—black men and women in captivity, who built the foundation of African American cultural life with their religious songs of joy, hope, pain, and suffering.

If a commitment to poststructuralism means that the African American religious voice must be hidden, then it is too high a price to pay, for this also obscures the most deeply held meanings of these African American authors. Perhaps Baker and Gates write out of an ignorance of African American religious history; if so, then their lapse is understandable. If not, then they must justify their exclusion or distortion of the African American religious heritage in the development of cultural meanings of African American narrative styles.

Conclusion

Gates and Baker are to be commended for their obvious respect and use of black narrative sources in their critical enterprise, and black theologians should emulate this aspect of their work. However, they share the basic difficulty that also was exposed with black theologians, namely, that they use methodologies that obfuscate the meanings of black culture. This often is manifested by a dualistic methodology that separates politics or culture from religion. These dualistic positions do not understand African American religion and culture as a complex dialectical interaction that has developed black cultural categories from the materials of African and African American culture and the social situation of oppression.

Their reliance on Eurocentric theories does not allow them to accomplish their goal of establishing critical theories that are responsive to and derivative from black culture. Their need to restate black culture in Eurocentric terms makes it nearly impossible to create linkages with the black oppressed because these Eurocentric terms rely on the discourses of the powerful. The style of the discourse is so foreign to the self-understandings of the black community in form or semantics that the black community is not able to benefit from their insights.

If one of the goals of the black theology and black aesthetic movements was to empower oppressed black persons, then the use of academic discourses that signal to black persons a lack of empathy with their plight is an important barrier to black solidarity. This use of the discourse of the oppressor has been cited as a major factor in the black community's suspicion of academically trained ministers and theologians. Academically trained black ministers must prove to their congregations that they still can relate to them through the use of traditional black sermonic techniques and styles, for it is these forms that communicate to oppressed black persons that these religious leaders still can identify with the plight of the black community. This does not mean that all forms of academic discourses should be eliminated. However, these forms of discourse should be examined to determine whether they may not inadvertently silence the voice of the African American community.

Contemporary black literary critics Baker and Gates have made some important contributions to the development of a black narrative hermeneutic. Yet, they leave the promise unfulfilled because they attempt to interpret black culture with an uncritical or semi-uncritical use of the methodological perspectives of Western European canons of scholarship.[54]

I suggest here, as I did with the case of African American historians, that the strategies of earlier black literary critics who emphasized the structural features of African American religion and culture provide the most promising avenues for the further development of a black narrative hermeneutic. This hermeneutic of retrieval is an important step in the development of a black narrative hermeneutic that does justice to African American religion and culture.

An Analysis of *All God's Dangers* Based on the Spirituals

Sometimes I feel like a moanin' dove
Sometimes I feel like a moanin' dove
Sometimes I feel like a moanin' dove;
 Wring my hands an' cry, cry, cry,
 Wring my hands an' cry.

The previous chapters have suggested that the African American religious heritage has acted as a silent and taken-for-granted subtext that has been the hermeneutic principle for the black community in the development of African American religion and culture. This subtext has operated at a silent level because of America's insensitivity and antipathy toward all things black and African, an antipathy often reproduced in the African American community itself. Yet, this silent subtext has continued to guide new forms of African American narrative expressions.

Spirituals have been a frame of reference for black action by serving as a goal for individual character development and social community action. Spirituals serve as a guide for a way of life that exhibits or embodies their principles. My argument is that people and groups become judged by the critical norms generated and found in spirituals.

For instance, with Martin Luther King Jr. as an example, one could ask if his life and work achieved the character of spirituals. Did King's nonviolent philosophy reveal a concern for diversity, an ability to improvise in the rhythm of protest? Did he show himself to be in contact with a personal God who guided him in his greatest moment of concern and fear? Did King articulate the struggle for civil rights and his opposition to the Vietnam War in the linguistic framework of family and freedom, thereby making himself understood and accepted by the black community?

The perspective of spirituals asserts that the most important experiences of King's life were gained in the dialectical context and interaction of faith and feeling, family and freedom. The famous kitchen experience is a narrative testimony to the powerful transmission of the spirituals process. The perspective of the spirituals can be seen as King relates this experience in *Stride Toward Freedom*:

> One night toward the end of January I settled into bed late, after a strenuous day. Coretta had already fallen asleep and just as I was about to doze off the telephone rang. An angry voice said, "Listen, nigger, we've taken all we want from you; before next week you'll be sorry you ever came to Montgomery." I hung up, but I couldn't sleep. It seemed that all of my fears had come down on me at once. I had reached the saturation point.
>
> I got out of bed and began to walk the floor. I was ready to give up. With my cup of coffee sitting untouched before me I tried to think of a way to move out of the picture without appearing a coward. In this state of exhaustion, when my courage had all but gone, I decided to take my problem to God. With my head in hands, I bowed over the kitchen table and prayed aloud. The words I spoke to God that midnight are still vivid in my memory. "I am here taking a stand for what I believe is right. But now I am afraid. The people are looking to me for leadership, and if I stand before them without strength and courage, they too will falter. I am at the end of my powers. I have nothing left. I've come to the point where I can't face it alone."
>
> At the moment I experienced the presence of the Divine as I had never experienced Him before. It seemed as though I could hear the quiet assurance of an inner voice saying: "Stand up for righteousness, stand up for truth; and God will be at your side forever." Almost at once my fears began to go. My uncertainty disappeared. I was ready to face anything.[1]

Three nights later, King's house was bombed, but he was able to deal with the situation without panic and within the principles of the nonviolent movement.[2]

I believe that the ethics of other black leaders and movements would reveal similar narrative experiences which reveal an orientation to African American religion in which the themes and style of the spirituals are present. More important is the presence of this spirituals orientation, which has been persistent in the everyday and crisis experiences of African Americans.

The Spiritual as Classic and Master Metaphor

The purpose of this work is not to argue that the spiritual is the only mode or metaphor from the African American narrative experience that is useful for further study of black religion and culture. I do believe, however, that my review of the research on spirituals demonstrates that spirituals can lay claim to being the foundational texts of black religious folk narrative forms. African American spirituals have stood the test of time, and they have proven to be one of the most powerful narrative forms in which African Americans have encoded their deepest meanings. Spirituals are a "classic" in African American religion and therefore can serve as guides for African American theological interpretations.

Using a spirituals hermeneutic can add interpretive power in deciphering the meanings of black life. This life is inherently dialectical because blacks continue to live in a situation of political and cultural negation. This perspective views African American spirituals as the repository of metaphors in which the traditions of African and European people converged as African Americans created a coherent life world in which the appropriate metaphors to deal with life's sorrows and joys could be recalled or created, as needed.

Scholars who have attempted to interpret African American narration in its literary or performance forms without understanding the African American community's own normative theological and ethical criteria have rendered faulty judgments. This appraisal may also extend beyond the African American Christian community.

To determine whether a spirituals hermeneutic indeed has been operating in the lives of African Americans we must examine African American narratives to see whether the meanings of American Americans are disclosed by analysis based on the structural and metaphorical characteristics of spirituals.

This analysis evaluates and interprets these narratives by the presence of evidence of a dialectical perspective that reflects the cultural, political, and ethnocentric perspectives as they were outlined in chapter 1. These narratives should give evidence of some of the structures that were found in the African American spirituals by cultural-structural methodologists. Features such as creativity (improvisation and spontaneity), community (call-and-response or antiphonal patterns) and pluralism (polyrhythms) should be present in these narratives. Also, the analyst should look for the interplay of metaphoric action that involves the metaphors of faith and feeling and family and freedom and for an intimacy between the divine and natural creation. This theological matrix can serve as an interpretive grid for a spirituals-based analysis of African American narratives.

This type of analysis privileges the particular cultural patterns of African Americans. It does not claim a universalist perspective, and it is suspicious of cultural bias when so-called universals are applied to African American texts. The analyst may wish to engage these African American structures and metaphors with other modes of thought, but it is a position of a narrative theology based on spirituals that African American religion must first be viewed from the standpoint of African American religious norms.

Rapetalistic Oppression as Social Context

In chapter 1, I mentioned that spirituals were developed out of a situation of rapetalistic oppression. The metaphors of spirituals, especially the family metaphors, were produced within social situations that attacked the physical and moral integrity of black women and men and within the context of economic exploitation, an oppression often tinged with overtones of sexual violence and exploitation. This construct is important because it argues for the interrelatedness of various aspects of African American oppression and because it helps us understand why spirituals so often emphasized family themes.

African Americans' experience was marked by constant threats to the integrity of their families through the sale of family members or through sexual violence or coercion. Several sources chronicle this often overlooked factor that plagued the lives of the African American slave and free communities. *All God's Dangers* is one such commentary.

Black women and men experienced their deepest frustrations due to their inability to control their bodies. This lack of bodily control also involved the world of work, where the economic control of black bodies for labor was the central concern of slavery and of the sharecropping system under which Nate Shaw lived.

The system of chattel slavery and racial discrimination was linked with such other social and bodily functions as sexuality, procreation, and parental control—areas that fundamentally involve the family. Spirituals were created when slaveowners reserved the right to preempt blacks' freedom in these fundamental areas of human life. African American women often were raped by slave owners and overseers or were forced to mate with black men according to the wishes of slaveowners in order to increase their "stock" of slaves. Historian Deborah Gray White reflects on the image of the black woman as Jezebel, the sexual temptress, during the slave period:

> The very sight of semiclad black women nurtured white male notions of their [black women's] promiscuity. Even the usually objective Frederick Law Olmsted, the famous Northern architect, had trouble avoiding the association. He stood for a long time watching slave women repair a road on a South Carolina plantation. The women had their coarse gray skirts "reefed up," around their waist and did no more than complete their assigned tasks. Nevertheless, Olmsted's impressions of them were distinctly negative. He described them as "clumsy," "gross," and "elephantine," yet added that in their demeanor the women were "sly," "sensual," and shameless." In the South, where it was not unusual for female slaves to work bent over with their skirts up, it was easy to come to such conclusions.[3]

During and after slavery, black males often found that castration was the punishment for real or imagined crimes against white society. This practice continued into the twentieth century.

A full recounting of the convergence of sexual, racial, and economic oppression is beyond the scope of this book, but note that attempts to reduce the scale of black suffering to primarily economic or racial categories depreciate the roles of sexuality, the family, and the body in the creation of African American cultural forms.[4]

It is no mistake, then, that many spirituals link themes of family and freedom. For African American slaves, freedom had to do not only with abstract formulations of justice but also with the right to develop a stable family life that was free from the possibility of sexual victimization and sudden dislocation. The context of rapetalistic oppression, in which black family life was under constant siege, prompted slaves to produce spirituals, which were narratives emphasizing the themes of family and freedom. These two themes are so related in spirituals that we can speak of the dialectic of family and freedom that continues to inform African American political interests. Nate Shaw's narrative gives readers the opportunity to examine this social process.[5]

Some black socialist theorists of the early nineteenth century wished to stress the linkages between the economic oppression of capitalism and the phenomenon of lynching. A. Philip Randolph, the famous leader of the Brotherhood of Sleeping Car Porters, discusses the plight of sharecroppers like Nate Shaw:

> Lynching, jim-crowism segregation is used to widen the chasm between the races.
>
> This profit system of capitalism also applies to the farmer through the crop-lien system. This is a system whereby a liken mortgage is taken upon the crops of the poor white and black farmers for a loan. . . .
>
> The farmer's inability to meet his note results in the loss of his farm. He then becomes a farm tenant and works upon the metayer system or the plan of giving a part of the crop produced to the owner for the privilege of cultivating the land. This crop lien system is profitable to the bankers of the South. Both white and black farmers are fleeced by this financial system. But white and black farmers won't combine against a common foe on account of race prejudice. Race antagonism, then is profitable to those who own the farms, the mills, the railroads, and the banks. This economic arrangement in the south is the fundamental cause of race prejudice, which is the fuse which causes the magazine of capitalism to explode into race conflicts—lynchings.[6]

Randolph asserts, therefore, that lynching primarily was a means by which capitalists controlled the lower classes and that the charge that lynchings were the just punishment of black men for sexual crimes committed against white women was a convenient excuse for this capitalist-inspired practice, which was designed to prevent lower-class blacks and whites from uniting against capitalist economic arrangements:

> To sum up, capitalism is at the basis of the economic, political and social arrangements of the South and it is defended, supported, promoted and upheld by the Republican and Democratic parties of the North, South,

East and West. Neither [the] Republican nor the Democratic party has ever condemned peonage or lynching. They can not. They are owned by the capitalists. . . .

. . . So that it is now a social habit to lynch Negroes. But when the motive for promoting race prejudice is removed, viz., profits, by the social ownership, control and operation of the machinery and sources of production through the government, the government being controlled by the workers, the effects of prejudice, race riots, lynching, etc., will also be removed.[7]

Therefore, in Randolph's view, once the socialist revolution occurs, the motive for racial discrimination and bias will be removed and lynchings will cease.

This orthodox Marxist position, which views cultural ideas as dependent on economic relations, does not acknowledge the power of a cultural ideology to continue on its own terms. The narrative of Nate Shaw seems to suggest that in the black community there was a belief that these oppressive ideologies not only were linked but also had a life of their own. I do not mean to deny the power of a Marxist analysis to uncover hidden economic motives for racist domination. However, in the narrative of Nate Shaw and in spirituals, we can see how the black community viewed these as interrelated phenomena and not as something that can be reduced to any of its component parts.

It now is necessary to test this position by applying it to an African American narrative. The narrative of King was a brief example, but let us turn now to a more extensive narrative that is particularly reflective of the African American religious experience.

African American Narrative Hermeneutics

To demonstrate the disclosive power of a narrative interpretation that originates within the meaning system of African Americans, I will examine the narrative *All God's Dangers: The Life of Nate Shaw*.[8]

We have Nate Shaw's life in a big book, every word of it his own. And we have a major figure that has been missing (by no accident) from the American consciousness for more than a century: the strong, tough, autonomous, powerful, rural Southern black man, self-possessed, ego intact, a whole man, unbroken by a system whose every purpose was to exploit, shatter and destroy him. We have more. We have a black Faulkner (and what an appropriate irony it is that Faulkner's black counterpart should prove, if only in the most technical sense of the word, to be illiterate— about as illiterate as Homer!) describing that black tenant farmer's world.[9]

Metaphors in Motion

Faith, Family, and Freedom

Going to see my mother some of these mornings,
　See my mother some of these mornings,
　See my mother some of these mornings,
　　Look away in the heaven
　　Look away in the heaven
　　Hope I'll join the band.

Shaw never understood the philosophical presuppositions of the Marxist-inspired movement in terms that political theorists would find satisfactory. He knew only that its emphasis on freedom was similar to the philosophy he had heard from his Grandmother Cealy and his community.

O My Lord Delivered Daniel
　O Daniel; O, Daniel,
O My Lord delivered Daniel
O Why not deliver me too?

There's a secret in this union somewhere and I ain't never understood it. They talked to me about it, that this union come from across the waters, and they called it a "soviet union." . . .

It was a thing that I never did thoroughly understand and get the backgrounds of it, but I was man enough to favor its methods. My head and heart had been well-loaded about the condition and the welfare of the poor—I couldn't stand it no more. I jumped in that organization and my name rings in it today. I haven't apologized to my Savior for joining; it was workin' for right. A man had to do it.[10]

This passage reveals that the African American religious community has implicit ideas about the relevance of theories of liberation but that theories must be stated in ways that are understandable and congruent with the meanings found in the spirituals theology of African Americans.

Shaw's grandmother, who survived slavery, was convinced that one day blacks were going to be free in America as they once were in Africa.

In Shaw's social context, the most powerful workers for black freedom were the Sharecropper's Union, a Marxist-inspired group. Shaw's passage reveals how African Americans in the early part of the twentieth century were attracted to socialist movements because they advocated black civil and human rights. As Shaw puts it, "I haven't apologized to my Savior for joining it." This juxtaposition of the sacred with a decidedly secular philosophy of social change reveals how African Americans became creators of political philosophies that were critical of social oppression without sacrificing their religious worldview.

Family and Freedom: The Political Dialectic

> Sometimes I feel like a motherless child
> Sometimes I feel like a motherless child
> Sometimes I feel like a motherless child
>   A long, long, way from my home.

Shaw's father was known for his violent temper and physical punishment of his wives and children:

> If I had a twenty-dollar bill this mornin for every time I seed my daddy beat up my mother and beat up my stepmother I wouldn't be settin here this mornin because I'd have up in the hundreds of dollars. Each one of them women—I didn't see no cause for it. I don't expect it ever come in my daddy's mind what his children thought about it or how they would remember him for it, but that was a poor example, to stamp and beat up children's mothers right before em.[11]

Shaw was in a lifelong battle to explain his father's behavior. His father experienced fifteen years of slavery before Emancipation: " 'Hayes was fifteen years old when it surrendered.' He was imprisoned in slavery for fifteen years—slavery were equal or worser than prison, but both of em bad and the poor colored man knows more about them two subjects than anybody."[12]

Shaw also talked about his father's lack of care concerning his actions, which Shaw likened to mental slavery: "My daddy was a free man but in his acts he was a slave. Didn't look ahead to pront hisself in nothin that he done. Is it or not a old slave act? Anything a man do in a slum way and don't care way. I just lap it right back on slavery time days. It's that old back yonder 'ism.' Slavery just taught the colored man to take what come and live for today. And the colored man held his children back as he held hisself.''[13]

Shaw's father was known in the community for his disdain for work and for his love of women, a love that produced four "outside" children:

> That was four outside children and that bout gets all of em. My daddy was one of these—O, I knows too much, I knowed more than a child oughta knowed in them days. Never did know my daddy boast about his outside children in front of his wives. He'd drop his head when they'd begin to shove them acts on him, he'd drop his head. My dear lovin mother never come up with such a thing as that against her as to have a young-un by an outside man; it never come up against TJ's mother to have young-un by a outside man.''[14]

In this passage, it is obvious that Shaw's father violated the Christian moral standard of monogamy and, obviously so, by the mothers of these "outside children" who were Nate's father's women. In a certain sense, however, discretion was the operative family ethic, a family ethic that has more in common with an African sense of polygamy or multiple relationships. Shaw's father did not boast about his sexual exploits. In fact, this seemed to be the only area in which he expressed the least amount of shame for his actions.

Rapetalistic Oppression   An analysis of Nate Shaw's life and thought that is based on spirituals must be aware of the role of women and the family in his development. The social context of rapetalistic oppression was particularly destructive to the African American family. Much of the struggle for black liberation and the evidence of the destructive social context can be found in the family milieu. In Shaw's conversation with one of his prison guards, this ideology was linked in very practical ways and often meant life and death for members of the black community:

> We was standin there by the fire talkin and he said to me, "Nate they electrocuted two Negroes at Kilby last night."
> . . . "Captain, what's that all about?"
> He said, "Well, rapin a white woman."
> ". . . But tell me, Captain, did they really do like they was accused of doin?"

"Aw hell, Nate"—dropped his head when he spoke—"I'll tell you the way that goes, Niggers and white women has been doin that for the longest and runnin together. Whenever a white woman, if she been foolin with a nigger, as soon as she finds out that she's in a little danger of bein found out, she goin to jump up and squall and holler. Nigger's burnt up then."[15]

In the next passage, Nate discusses the sexual coercion exercised by this same prison guard in relation to the black women prisoners: "I come to find out that Captain Locke would take them colored gals out from the prison department—and there was nothin to a white man but to do that. When they'd check them colored women out there for farm work—choppin cotton and hoein cotton and rakin out ditches—this fellow Locke would take a chance with some of em."[16] Shaw goes on to relate how one black male prisoner complained about this guard's treatment of the black women to the point that Captain Locke had this prisoner transferred to another prison. Locke later was dismissed by the prison warden because of his familiarity with the black prisoners.

These passages reveal how the realities of economic, sexual, and racial oppression are interrelated in the black community. In this case, the nature of the oppression was not just economic or racial (i.e., the oppression of blacks under the capitalist system) but also involved issues of sexual violence and exploitation that affected black men and women in gender-specific ways. Black men were often accused of rape and summarily jailed and executed. Black women were often victims of rape and sexual abuse.

The narrative response of African Americans found in spirituals recognizes this state of affairs. African American spirituals, with their tremendous emphasis on family themes, are cries of anguish and hope about this situation of rapetalistic oppression:

> I'm a poor, wayfaring stranger,
> While journeying through this world of woe,
>   Yet there's no sickness, toil and danger,
> In that bright world to which I go.

Shaw's family life was marked by ambiguity. On the one hand, his relationship with the women in his family was positive and loving. On the other hand, he had difficulty negotiating a stable relationship as an adult.

There's a man going round taking names,
There's a man going round taking names,
   He's a-taken my mother's name,
   And he's left my heart in pain,
There's a man going round taking names.

Shaw retells his relationship to his mother in glowing terms. His mother regularly sacrificed her own needs for her children's safety, but unfortunately she died while Shaw was a young child. After his mother's death, his grandmother provided a stable source of support for him. However, neither his mother or grandmother was able to protect her children from Nate's father's brutal assaults:

My mother's name was Liza; she was Liza Culver. She was a deep yaller woman—her mother was a half-white woman. Her mother and daddy died before I was born. . . .
   Good God, them two boys and my mother practically done all the field work. My mother especially done anything my daddy told her to do as far as cultivatin a crop out there—I seed her do it—that a man ought to done. She'd plow, she'd hoe; and my daddy'd tell her. "Take that plow!" "Hoe!" And here's the way I seed her go many a day, and that was a every year's job for her. My daddy'd have his gun on his shoulder and be off an Sitmachas Creek swamps, huntin. And her and her little brothers would be in the field at work. She'd be out there with her dress rolled up nearly to her knees, just so she could have a clear stroke walkin. Pushed up and rolled up around her waist and string tied around it and her dress would bunch up around her hips. She'd be in the field workin like a man, my daddy out in the woods somewhere huntin.[17]

Going to see my mother some of these mornings.
  see my mother some of these mornings,
  see my mother some of these mornings,
    Look away in the heaven
    Hope I'll join the band.

It was the women in Nate's life who held to the moral standards of monogamy while they accepted the children of Nate's father's unions without bitterness expressed toward the children. The children were not penalized for the father's unfaithfulness or the mother's indiscretions. Shaw was to duplicate his father's sexual behavior.

Shaw viewed his father's destructive acts as a continuation of a slave mentality that was particularly destructive to the family. At one point in his life, Shaw had an opportunity for schooling, but Shaw's father prevented it from happening:

> There was a preacher used to come out of Tuskegee down there. His name, his initials was BB, BB Fletcher. He used to travel through right by our home when I was a boy. And he'd stop and visit with us on his way to Somerset, Alabama, to a colored church up there. . . .
>
> He wanted my daddy to give me up, let me get off to where I could get a better chance and have better treatment. Probably I would have let one of mine go off since I've looked through that thing as I have. Preacher Fletcher told my daddy. "Brother Shaw, let me have him, I see somethin in him. If you let me have him I'll let him learn any kind of trade he wants to learn, if you'll just give him to me."[18]

Shaw's father refused to allow him to attend Tuskegee because he wanted to keep Shaw working for him. This passage reveals the role of the black minister as an advocate for the advancement of the black family through educational missionary efforts. However, Nate Shaw was not permitted to take advantage of this opportunity because of his father's shortsightedness. Shaw missed the opportunity to learn a trade at the famous institution founded by Booker T. Washington.

> I woke up this morning with my mind,
>   Stayed on freedom. . . .
> My mother got her mind,
>   Stayed on freedom. . . .
> Hallelu! Hallelu! Hallelu!

In spite of the negative experiences with his father, Shaw found nurturing and moral and religious guidance from the women in his family. He learned about faith and freedom from within the nexus of his family's love as it was transmitted through his mother's and grandmother's stories and experiences:

> I didn't know what it was to suffer while my mother lived. So far as somethin' to eat. I din't know what it was to go hungry in my lifetime. . . . But after my mother died I knowed what it was to eat only dry bread or put it in water and mash it up. . . . It really wasn't a change in my

daddy, he was already providin' only when it suited him. But my mother would take food from her own dinner and reserve it for her children. But after she died, if there was anything a little nourishin' or tasty, I din't get it and the rest of the children din't get it—my daddy would eat it up.[19]

Nate's participation in the Sharecroppers Union was an extension of the feeling of freedom he had gained from his family, especially his grandmother. From his family, he had developed a keen sense of justice in both its positive and negative terms. The injustice he suffered from his father did not leave him in despair; instead, he knew what justice was since he had received so little of it from the most important male figure in his life. Nate became a leader of the movement in his town and suffered a false imprisonment as one of the activist leaders of his community:

The Bible says, "What has been will be again," and Grandma Cealy said a right smart about this; that that day was comin. Colored people once knowed what it was to live under freedom before they got over in this country, and they would know it again. That this very freedom move-ment that's on now would come. I heard them words and I was old enough to understand. And when I got to be a little boy, when I got big enough to catch on to what people said, and even to the words of the old people, and the Bible it was instilled in me many a time: the bottom rail will come to the top someday. I taken that to mean a change in the later years, durin of my lifetime maybe. I believe, if that day come, the poor generation on earth will banish away their toils an snares. But won't nobody do it for em but themselves. Take me, I'm a colored man. I've come in the knowledge of what it feels like to move out of this back yonder "ism"; and I'm confident all of my race will someday move out from under earthly bondage.[20]

In these passages, we see that Shaw learned about love at its deepest and most practical level: self-sacrifice in order to care for one's family and the hope for freedom as it was expressed by the African American religious interpretation of scripture. These themes are examples of a theology of the spirituals at work in the lives of the African American community as it was transmitted from one generation to the next.

There's a better day a-coming,
    Don't you get weary;
Oh, slap your hands, children,

Oh, pat your feet, children,
  Don't you get weary,
There's a great campmeeting in the promised land.

Spirituals view life as a dialectical situation in which faith and feeling, family and freedom are in constant tension. The most powerful expressions of African American religious life and action were developed—or, one might say, "conjured" up—as blacks sought to create a social world in which family relations were viewed as sacred and protected. The spirituals were the black religious response to this situation of rapetalistic oppression. If we are not to be guilty of academic imperialism, we must acknowledge the right of the black folk community to theorize about their own oppression.

Faith and Feeling: The Cultural Dialectic—African Ritual Structure

I got a mother in the bright shinin' world,
I got a mother in the bright shinin' world,
Dear mother, I hope to meet you over there
  in the bright shinin' world.

The feeling side of Shaw's life was forced underground by his father's brutality and his mother's death. To survive, Shaw had to steel himself against his father's brutality, and so he plunged himself into the world of work. He told about his courtship of his wife in a very matter-of-fact way. It was more like conducting a business agreement than like falling in love. Although Shaw resented his father's infidelity, he found himself reproducing his behavior:

She was a Christian girl when I married her. And she was a woman that wanted to keep as far as her hands and arms could reach, all the surrounding, she wanted to keep it clean. And I kept myself clean as I possible could. But in past days, I've sneaked about in places, I did. I own to my part of wrongness. Maybe I've had contact with other women, but not many, and I handled the proposition quiet. I liked other women, but it was just certain women that I liked. I din't pitch out there and run at every old woman or gal in the country after I married her—din't do it before that. And I desperately kept clean of runnin' too much to a extreme at other women when I had her. Regardless to all circumstances I weren't a man to slip around at women and no matter what I said to another or what I done, I felt my wife come first.[21]

Once again, Shaw reveals a sexual ethic of discretion—a compromise between the real and the ideal, between polygamy and monogamy—in the conduct of his sexual affairs. It exemplified a state of affairs vaguely reminiscent of an African past of multiple relationships and respect for various mates.

Shaw's emotional energies were directed toward his work, yet he found these energies expanded as he underwent a religious conversion during his arrest. Instead of some kind of universal norms of faith development, Shaw's conversion should be viewed within the context of an African American analysis based on spirituals. Looked at this way, it would be seen as a movement toward religious maturity, which in the black community means a religious development in which the capacities for faithful (i.e,. religious) feeling and acts of devotion to family and freedom would be actualized. In this perspective, the priestly and prophetic roles of religious devotion are connected in thought and action.

> Soon I'll be done with the trouble of this world,
> Soon I'll be done with the trouble of this world,
> Soon I'll be done with the trouble of this world,
>   Going to live with God.

Shaw's conversion represents an African American communal theological orientation in which religious experience serves to reintegrate the individual to community life through a transcendent experience. The play of these metaphors and structures of the spirituals can be seen in Shaw's conversion experience:

> The mornin' I was converted. I was walkin' around there in the jailhouse fixin' to shave. And I couldn't satisfy myself to save my life—walkin' around, leapin' everywhere, in a trance. I couldn't rest nowhere—they lookin' at me. And all of a sudden, God stepped in my soul. Talk about hollerin' and rejoicin', I just caught fire. My mind cleared up. I got so happy—I di'n't realize where I was at. I lost sight of this world to a great extent. And the Master commenced a talkin' to me just like a natural man. I heard these words plain—I dote on it, dote one my friends, too—the Lord spoke to me that mornin' said "Follow me and trust me for my holy righteous word, the devil can't do you no harm." Good God almighty, I just felt like I could have flown out the top of that jail. I commence a shoutin' 'bout the Lord, how good and kind and merciful He was. Freed my soul from sin. I was a raw piece of plunder that

mornin' in jail. God heard me and answered my prayers. Some of the worst fellows in there looked at me but they couldn't stand it, had to turn away, and their faces looked just as sad.[22]

I've been in the storm so long,
I've been in the storm so long, children,
I've been in the storm so long,
 Oh, give me little time to pray.
 Oh, let me tell my mother
How I come along,
With a hung down head and a aching heart,
 Oh, give me little time to pray.

In this conversion story, we see the convergence and play of the metaphors and structures of African American spirituals. Shaw was in emotional agony over the welfare of his family. He became emotionally affected to the extent that he could not remain still, and then he experienced the deepest joy that he had ever known.

This surplus of feeling is reminiscent of the style of spirituals DuBois and Hurston described, in which African Americans found their deepest feelings of anguish met by a religious presence that could transform their despair into hope. Conversion is not just a one-time affair but continually is relived as a part of the ongoing religious experience.

Call and Response

My soul is a witness for my Lord,
My soul is a witness for my Lord,
My soul is a witness for my Lord,
My soul is a witness for my Lord.

Shaw's conversion narrative also reveals the call-and-response pattern of Martin Luther King Jr.'s narrative, and which is normative in spirituals' style of improvisation, call and response, and polyrhythms. In the experience of the divine, God calls and humans respond, and God speaks to a person like "a natural man." This experience was so powerful that Shaw's fellow male prisoners could not bear to look at him in such a time of emotional nakedness.

Improvisation: Liminality and Communitas

> Walk together, children,
>   Don't you get weary,
> Walk together, children,
>   Don't you get weary,
> Oh, walk together, children,
>   Don't you get weary,
> There's a great camp meeting
>   In the Promised Land.

Shaw's religious conversion allowed him to relate more deeply to his wife and family. He seemed to be more sensitive to his responsibility for their particular situations. While in prison, he was able to continue to provide for his family both materially and emotionally, although his twelve-year absence still worked a great hardship on his family.

Shaw's religious experience helped him bear his prison sentence and keep in close touch with his family. He did not become embittered like his father. Instead, he continued to cultivate his newfound religious orientation, which was characterized by the metaphors and structures of spirituals.

Religious conversion in the African American community, as we see in the case of Nate Shaw, followed this West African pattern of disintegration-rejuvenation-reintegration. Shaw's conversion allowed him—and African American slaves before him—to be reborn into the African American mythic community ethos, which understood life to be a process of creation out of destruction.

This view of hope from despair also, of course, is a feature of evangelical Christianity, with its emphasis on resurrection from death. African Americans, with their sense of daily crucifixion due to oppressive circumstances, combined their African mythic sense with the traditional Christian experience in which religious conversion was the entry point and created this African and Christian mythic sensibility.

Shaw's life reveals an ability to adapt to particular situations. This ability to improvise is one of the key features of African and African American music and culture. The essence of the regenerative powers of the Spirit are symbolized by water.

> Wade in the water, children,
> Wade in the water, children,

Wade in the water, children,
  God's gonna trouble the water.

Shaw's story is important because it focuses attention on the narrative shape of the African American community. Rosengarten allows Shaw's story to be told in his own voice and with its inherent meanings. This story is filled with the meaning and energy of spirituals. Shaw resisted the coercion prevalent in his community and, in doing so, earned a twelve-year sentence in an Alabama jail. Yet it was in jail that Shaw, like other African American men before and after him, experienced religious conversion.

After his conversion Shaw had a friend write a letter to his wife, telling her of his experience and of his new relation to God:

> I had him tell her that God had answered my lonely calls. I had seeked my soul's salvation and found it. And she came bustin' in there when she got the letter just as quick as she could come. Shaw quotes his cellmate's report to his wife on the power of his conversion: "Mrs. Shaw, if there's ever been a man converted, Nate's one of 'em. She felt so good about that—she was cryin', she was so happy. She was a woman—she was a Christian girl when I married her and I was a sinner boy."[23]

When the storm of life is raging,
  Stand by me, stand by me.
When the world is tossing me,
Like a ship upon the sea,
Thou who rulest wind and water,
  Stand by me, stand by me.

I know my robe is gonna fit me well,
I tried it on at the gates of hell.

Shaw, his wife, and his friend were operating out of a value system informed by the meanings of spirituals, a theological orientation that valued faith and feeling, family and freedom.

The Psychological Dialectic

Shaw's narrative also reflects the psychological dialectic in which the black community has no recognition that they are engaging in African-based cultural practices. Shaw and his community are aware of themselves only as Negroes of American origin with a Christian religious perspective.

This lack of African cultural awareness reveals how thoroughly African Americans were deprived of a working knowledge of their own cultural heritage because of the European American ethnocentric biases in the United States. I hope that my analysis of spirituals and of Shaw's religious perspective illustrates how integral African religious and cultural ideas were to the development and practices of the African American community.

Neither Shaw nor the African American community should be blamed for this lack of knowledge. The first and foremost goal of the black community has always been to survive. One can only wonder whether a fuller knowledge and appreciation of their cultural background would have aided them in their psychological and social struggles.

> Soon I'll be done with the trouble of this world,
> Soon I'll be done with the trouble of this world,
> Soon I'll be done with the trouble of this world,
>   Going to live with God.

It is impossible to read the African American spirituals and not be impressed with the tremendous range of their sensibilities and emotions. Readers are also overwhelmed with a sense of the genius of these "unknown bards" who expressed in simple yet elegant terms the fundamental desires of the human spirit. No word was wasted as these poets spoke about their world of joy and pain. As long as African American life is hampered by racism and discrimination, spirituals will speak in all their fullness to this life situation.

Spirituals, in effect, are the foundation for the blues. Explicitly religious language cannot speak all meanings, for it is hampered by social conventions and implicit notions of what is morally appropriate subject matter. However, the religious language of the spirituals created a surplus of meaning that led to the development of other black musical forms. The church member who moaned on Sunday would, more than the church would like to admit, sing the blues on Saturday. Not until the advent of gospel music in the early twentieth century did spirituals and the blues reached a musical compromise.

Spirituals and the blues are inextricably linked, but they express distinct life situations and energies. The blues are not simply secular spirituals, nor are spirituals religious blues. They are distinct but related musical forms that articulate different areas of the human soul. They both express the souls of black folk.[24]

African American religion generated an ethics of caring. The corporate body's experience of the divine in worship and devotion built faith through intense feeling, both corporately and individually. This religious experience laid the foundation for acts of caring for the family and for political freedom. Persons and communities who evidenced these virtues and experiences were deemed spiritually mature. Nate and his community exemplified this perspective, which laid the foundation for the greatest movement for freedom in this country: the civil rights movement and its heroes and sheroes.

Spiritual Reflections on *The Song of Solomon* and *Beloved*

It would be impudent for me to criticize such splendid scholars as Baker and Gates without showing how a critique based on the spirituals could function in the analysis of African American literature. For that purpose, I will explore the work of the most celebrated African American novelist of our era, Toni Morrison.

The spirituals' themes of faith and feeling, family and freedom are ever present in her novels. These four themes, as I have argued earlier, comprise the matrix of African American religion and culture that were prominent in our analysis of the Negro spirituals. I believe they also are themes within which Morrison weaves her magic.

Her earlier novels, such as *The Bluest Eye*,[25] *Sula*,[26] and *Tar Baby*,[27] also were concerned with family interactions and the quest for freedom in the context of the social and psychological oppression of African Americans. However, her most celebrated works, *The Song of Solomon*[28] and *Beloved*,[29] construct an African world that is particularly potent.

My contention is that Morrison's work is especially representative of African American religion and culture because its themes and its style reflect the matrix of the spirituals. This matrix includes Christianity but

extends far beyond sectarian religious divisions to a profound understanding of African cultural structures.

Song of Solomon

Family and Freedom

The plot of *Song of Solomon* involves a young black man's search for
identity. Milkman Dead, son of the town's most powerful black citizen,
Macon Dead, is a rootless young man interested only in realizing his
own selfish ambitions for material and physical gratification. He has
been terribly spoiled by his mother. The name Milkman was given to
him by a character who accidentally viewed his mother breastfeeding
him at a later than usual age. He is the bane of his family due to his
cavalier attitude toward life.

Milkman is interested in gaining wealth by any means possible, even
stealing from his own Aunt Pilate. Anything would be better than earn-
ing his livelihood in the cold, hard way of work and stinginess that his
father exemplifies. Milkman's awakening to his cultural roots occurs
during his quest for lost gold that he supposes is kept by his aunt. His
Aunt Pilate represents a time of African root healers and spiritual diviners. He believes that the bag she carries with her is full of gold, and he
and his friend Guitar attempt to steal it.

Eventually he discovers that the bag does not contain gold but instead
holds the bones of Pilate and Macon's father, something much more
valuable than the gold Milkman had been seeking. In his quest for
riches, Milkman has to travel south to his American ancestral home of
Virginia. In the backwoods of Virginia, Milkman begins to make connections between his present and his past, connections that eventually
give him a sense of pride and purpose.

Morrison's situating the story in the family and Milkman's quest,
resulting in the rediscovery of his family, reveal the spiritual dialectic of
family and freedom. Pilate represents an archetypical African cultural
presence that has been lost to Milkman's generation. The ethnocentric
dialectic by which all things black and African have been disdained and
hidden from the conciousness of African Americans has worked to develop young people who have no sense of ancestral worship or communal values.

Milkman and his father, Macon, represent the black quest for American materialism at any cost, and his friend Guitar, although anxious to use the lost gold to further black retaliation against white oppression, does not understand the true meaning of black love and compassion.

The African cultural understanding of family runs strongly through Morrison's work. In this world family includes the dead, the ancestors that went before. The family's name—Dead—describes their spiritual state, but it also is a sign of the inclusion of those who have gone before. Both major female characters, his mother, Ruth, and his Aunt Pilate, are in constant communication with their dead fathers. They understand their lives to be intricately connected to their dead relatives and their living children.

Faith and Feeling

Africosmysticism* is a theme that runs throughout Morrison's novels. She demonstrates what the ethnocentric dialectic attempts to cover up, namely, that the African worldview remains a present reality in much of African American religion and culture. The ancestral spirits still speak to Protestant African American Christians who have lost the intricate and detailed knowledge of Africa because of the repression of slavery. The exact words of incantation that invoke these spirits may be gone, but they nonetheless appear.

Morrison's work examines the intricate way that the black family is affected by the sociopolitical circumstances of racism and oppression. The matrix of rapetalistic oppression is a constant partner in the shaping of black family life. The family is the most severely affected by this oppressive matrix, but in the family some measure of freedom is gained. Milkman and his family gain a greater sense of joy and peace through their reconnection with their family in Virginia. Their return to Virginia completes a circle that had been broken in their move to northern climes. The sociopolitical situation has not changed, but the family now is much stronger and able to meet the challenges that rapetalistic oppression offers.

---

*My term for the depths of African spirituality.

The climax of *Song of Solomon* reveals the depth of feeling that forms the central core of African American religious faith. Milkman's spiritual liberation comes as he is able to expand his emotional life to include a genuine caring for the people in his life, illustrated in his relationship to a female prostitute who grants him hospitality during his Southern travels. Where before he had a cavalier, unfeeling attitude toward women, an attitude that resulted in the death of his cousin Hagar, he now shows genuine caring for Sweet, a woman who has treated him with kindness in both body and soul despite her status as a "working girl." Their lovemaking is a real sharing of spirit not confined to the act of copulation. For probably the first time in his life, Milkman ministers to the physical, spiritual, and economic needs of someone else.

The closer he gets to his ancestral secret, the more humane and human he becomes. The culmination of Milkman's journey comes when he deciphers the history of his family, which is directly descended from the legendary flying Africans who had the ability to ride the winds back to the freedom of Africa's shores.

The novel ends with Milkman's life being threatened by his best friend, Guitar, who has become so crazed to recover the gold that doesn't exist that he shoots and kills Pilate and is ready to shoot Milkman. In this moment, Milkman discovers the true extent and meaning of freedom, first from Pilate in her dying words—"I wished I'd knowed more people. I would of loved em all"—and then existentially as he surrenders to the air, leaps, and "flies" to meet his killer. In this last act, which for Milkman is his first act of faith, he finds the true nature of African spirituality, a surrender to the spiritual heritage of his ancestors.

The African cultural postmodern sensibility also is an integral feature of Morrison's work *Beloved.* This attitude of African mysticism by which she ends both *Song of Solomon* and *Tar Baby* becomes the focus for the entire book in *Beloved.* In this work, the unfulfilled ancestor that reincarnates itself into the family that has wronged it is Beloved itself.[30]

Rapetalistic Oppression

Morrison graphically portrays the destructive extent of rapetalistic oppression. She shows how the modern worldview—with its emphasis on the control of the body of African captives on the plantation, the prison system, and even in the so-called freedom of the North—distorts the possibilities of family and freedom. Morrison shows how rape, bestiality, and other forms of sexual abuse result from the American slave system. Her depiction of the male homosexual rape scenes in the prison system[31] and the bestiality by black male slaves without sexual partners shows a perceptive awareness of how the system of slavery also affected the sexual functioning of black men. The stealing of Sethe's milk by her captors is a powerful metaphor for a system that controlled the bodies of black females and offered little respect for them. This system had a destructive power so devastating that it led some women like Sethe to commit infanticide rather than have their daughters exist within that same system.

Beloved exists as a promise, the culmination of a black literature that fully depicts the rapetalistic horror of black slavery. Other novels have treated black slavery, but none has done it with such power and with such attention to the African mystical sensibility. David Bradley's *The Chaneysville Incident*[32] probably came the closest, but, like Morrison's other works, the African worldview is fully expressed or hinted at only in the closing pages. *Beloved,* however, weaves the African cultural view throughout the text by positioning the main character as an ancestral spirit returned from the dead.

Beloved

Family and Freedom

Once again, the black family is the site for the story. *Beloved* chronicles the history of a black family in America. It depicts the everyday existence of slavery and tells the lives of some of its members who were able to make the treacherous trip to "freedom" in the North. The novel shows how all-consuming this hope for freedom for one's family was in the African captive community. Attempts to escape or buy oneself from captivity are the main goals of slave families. Morrison shows just how difficult this proposition was and the great lengths to which family members were willing to go to make it a reality. Baby Suggs, Sethe's mother-in-law, gave birth to eight children by six fathers but was allowed to keep only her last child, Halle, as a kind of compensation for the master's need to sell her children who had not died in infancy.[33]

Faith and Feeling

Beloved also shows the postmodern emphasis on a spirituals-based religion, a religion characterized by the experience of black women who have a connection with God's world. Baby Suggs is in the tradition of African women's leadership, and, as she invokes the spirit in the clearing, others come to join her in worship. This novel evokes the depth of the African religious experience. Life is met with deep feeling and empathy. Faith is not separated from life but is an expression of life itself. The love a mother has for her son—"A man ain't nothing but a man," Baby Suggs said, "But a son? Well now, that's somebody"[34]—is a divine gift. The love between women and men is much more difficult to accomplish, but this quest for relationship is the underlying motif of the book.

Readers wonder whether Paul D and Sethe will be able to overcome the impact of rapetalistic oppression and find each other. Will they overcome their own past and the hurts and pains caused by modernity's shackles, or will they eventually drift apart? They call to God not in the formal moments of church services but in the midst of despair. Their lives are like spirituals, stories of faith and feeling that trust in the power of truth (spirit) to set them free.

Rapetalistic Oppression and African American Spirituals–Based Ethics

Spirituals represent what I call the "ethics of discretion," which involves both an emphasis on building strong traditional families and a silence on sexual matters due to issues of personal privacy and cultural safety. The black church continues to promote the spirituals-based sexual ethic, while the media and the entertainment industry have tended to promote an ethic more reminiscent of the blues, an ethic that celebrates sexuality and the body.

African Americans do not participate exclusively in one or the other sexual ethic. In fact, there is significant interchange between the two ethical orientations. It almost has become a cliché that most popular rhythm-and-blues artists had their start in the church, singing spirituals and gospel music. Just as there has been mutual participation in both musical spheres, the same can be said of the interchange of sexual ethical orientations, as we will see in the life of Nate Shaw.

This community of Africans in America was born between the spirituals and the blues, as this slave testimony of Old Elizabeth in 1772 signifies:

> In the eleventh year of my age, my master sent me to another farm, several miles from my parents, brothers and sisters, which was a great trouble to do. At last I grow so lonely and sad I thought I should die, if I did not see my mother. I asked the overseer if I might go, but being positively denied, I concluded to go without his knowledge. When I reached home my mother was away. I set off and walked twenty miles before I found her. I staid with her for several days, and we returned together. Next day I was sent back to my new place, which renewed my sorrow. At parting, my mother told me that I had "nobody in the wide world to look to but God." These words fell upon my heart with wondrous weight, and seemed to add to my grief. I went back repeating as I went, "none but God in the wide world." On reaching the farm, I found the overseer was displeased at me for going without his liberty. He tied me with a rope, and gave me some stripes of which I carried the marks for weeks."[35]

Old Elizabeth later found God, and it was her conversion that allowed her to live with the blue note of American chattel slavery.

This modulation between the spirituals and the blues has resulted in more than a little confusion among African Americans about the nature of their ethical responses in the New World. This confusion is compounded by the role of sexual stereotyping and the history of the sexual exploitation of African Americans.

In the black church, while it still is acceptable to move the body and express one's joy of the Lord through bodily expression, too much movement makes middle-class black churches uneasy, for it reminds them of their status as African slaves. In lower-economic-class churches, which are not as sensitive to the dominant culture's negative stereotyping, this movement can even take the form of dancing, shouting, and a general falling out on the floor. Try as one might, it is difficult not to be aroused both physically and spiritually by the sight of bodies moving and swaying to the power of the Spirit.

Likewise with the blues: Even though they speak in raw terms of the common, everyday situations that afflict black people, they are also ethical laments on a world gone mad. Ethics ultimately are derived from a religious sense of divine order and justice. Therefore, when the blues person cries to the Lord over the injustice of love gone wrong or over the pain of social injustice, it is a heartfelt cry of the spirit that can move grown men to cry.

Instead of viewing black theology and ethics either as an unbroken string from Africa or as a completely new African American creation, we must consider the theology and ethics of African Americans as the result of both the African past and the American experience of oppression.

This sexually influenced oppression by Europeans and Americans of Africans continues to have a devastating effect on the psyche and social nature of Americans, black and white alike. The purpose of rapetalistic oppression was to inculcate in the slaves' minds a sense of powerlessness over their own bodies. They were kept at dis-ease over the status of their bodies. They had little choice over their own sexuality and the choice of their sexual partners because the final decision over slave marriages had to be approved by the master. They could be sold from their families and social group at any time, which meant that they never could feel completely comfortable in their social setting. In the back of their minds, they recognized that they could be sold at any time. They were designated as objects: bodies without souls or feelings. Many slave testimonies emphasize the sense of despair over both the possibility and actuality of slaves being sold away from family and friends.

The early sexual stereotyping of African Americans by Europeans and Americans is well documented. It involved the development of sexual stereotypes of both men and women. Black people were said to possess sexual instincts that were savage in nature. The physiognomy of black males and females was thought to be unusual. In America, where blacks were bred to increase slave capital, the sexual myths of black men as stud horses and black women as wanton jezebels were used to justify the rapacious sexual and economic motives of white slaveowners. Sexual exploitation of African women was the rule of the day for much of America's cultural history.

The desired result of rapetalistic oppression was to create an ethic among the slaves that was in keeping with the slavemasters' needs. Convincing black men and women that they were, indeed, nothing more than studs and jezebels would make the masters' task that much easier. Slavemasters, however, also had to believe their own hype. The ideology that constructed the sexuality of the slaves also constructed the sexuality of the slavemasters. This made possible the transference of their own sexual desires and prohibitions onto the African body. White women became the virtuous property of white men, and they were not allowed to enjoy their sexuality lest they be likened to "niggers." White "civilized" sexuality used the otherness of Africans to define its own sexuality. The so-called Victorian sexuality can be seen as the direct result of the construction of a sexuality that was "other"—other than that of the "uncivilized" natives of two-thirds of the world.

In the black community, this process often has resulted in internalized oppression, which occurs when the oppressed group begins to accept and act out the values that have been imposed upon them by the dominant group. One index of the success of this ideology in the black community is the proliferation of wanton sexual images portrayed in the music videos of black urban youth. Unlike the sexual cleverness that marks blues music, rap videos often replace artistry with a sexual explicitness that reduces black men and women to bodies without souls.

This cultural attitude of rapetalistic oppression in which racial, sexual, and economic exploitations converge has served to intensify racist attitudes. I believe that the treatment of blacks has set a psychological tone in America in which sexual abuse has become a way of life. Sexual abuse is America's dirty little secret that surfaces only with spectacular trials such as the Menendez, Simpson, or Bobbit affairs.

Muthufucka Is More Than a Word

It is no mistake that the most powerful, frequently used, and characteristic epithet of the black community is the sexually based "muthufucka." This epithet harkens back to the racial memory that persists in the black community as a defining ethical and social moment. Whites have no idea of the continuing psychic trauma caused to blacks by the rape of black mothers—their motherfucking—and the forced sexual mating of black men and women during colonial and pre–Civil War times. This historical memory has great psychological power and keeps alive the black community's awareness of its "bastard" social and economic status in America.

The film *The Journey of August King* depicts the tragic depths of rapetalistic oppression. August King is an ordinary white North Carolina farmer in 1815 who comes upon a young female runaway slave. King is confronted by the slaveowner, who is extremely upset over the loss of his slave. It turns out that this runaway slave, who is his personal household attendant, also is his daughter. It is painfully obvious that the slaveowner has more than a father's love for his runaway slave daughter, Annalisa. This incestuous exploitation of one's own family members has contributed to the psychological power of American chattel slavery. Even if the slaveowner did not have sex with his daughter, a question that the film begs, the slave girl states that she needs to gain her freedom in order to save her soul. Her freedom from slavery means freedom from her father's psychological and physical (i.e., rapetalistic) domination.

This film has one of the goriest sights possible, a black male runaway slave hung upside down naked, as was the custom when black slaves were punished—or more accurately tortured—for their rebellion. The slaveowner, with an axe in his hand, in a fit of anger slices the black slave in two like a side of beef.

The slave narratives of the WPA Federal Writers Project are full of slave testimonies concerning the stripping and brutal torture of black slaves:

> My old master was Dave Gile, the meanest man that ever lived. He didn't have many slaves—my mammy, and me, and my sister, Uncle Bill, and Truman. He had owned my grandma, but he give her a bad whupping, and she never did git over it and died. We all done as much work as a dozen niggers—we knowed we had to.
>
> I seen Old Master git mad at Truman, and he buckled him down across a barrel and whupped him till he cut the blood out of him, and then he rubbed salt and pepper in the raw places. It looked like Truman would die, it hurt so bad. I know that don't sound reasonable that a white man in a Christian community would do such a thing, but you can't realize how heartless he was. People didn't know about it, and we dasn't tell for we knowed he'd kill us if we did. You must remember he owned us body and soul, and they wasn't anything we could do about it. Old Mistress and her three girls was mean to us too.[36]

> My father took me away from my mother at age of six weeks old and gave me to my grandmother who was real old at the time. Just before she died, she gave me back to my father, who was my mammy's master. He was a old bachelor and run a saloon, and he was white, but my mammy was a Negro. He was mean to me.

Finally my father let his sister take me and raise me with her children. She was good to me, but before he let her have me he willed I must wear a bell till I was twenty-one year old, strapped round my shoulders with the bell 'bout three feet from my head in a steel frame. That was for punishment for being born into the world a son of a white man and my mammy, a Negro slave. I wears this frame with the bell where I couldn't reach the clapper, day and night. I never knowed what it was to lay down in bed and get a good night's sleep till I was 'bout seventeen year old, when my father died and my sister took the bell offen me.

Before my father gave me to his sister, I was tied and strapped to a tree and whipped like a beast by my father, till I was unconscious, and then left strapped to a tree all night in cold and rainy weather. My father was very mean. He and he sister brung me to Texas, to North Zulch, when I 'bout twelve year old. He brung my mammy, too, and made her come and be his mistress one night every week. He would have kilt every one of his slaves rather than see us go free, 'specially me and my mammy.[37]

She didn't work in the field. She worked at a loom. She worked so long and so often that once she went to sleep at the loom. Her master's boy saw her and told his mother. His mother told him to take a whip and wear her out. He took a stick and went out to beat her awake. He beat my mother till she woke up. When she woke up, she took a pole out of the loom and beat him nearly to death with it. He hollered, "Don't beat me no more, and I won't let 'em whip you."

She said, "I'm going to kill you. These black titties sucked you, and then you come out here to beat me." And when she left him, he wasn't able to walk.

And that was the last I seen of her until after freedom. She went out and got on an old cow that she used to milk—Dolly, she called it. She rode away from the plantation, because she knew they would kill her if she stayed.[38]

I have watched with great pain and anguish the continuing effects of slavery on my black students as they have worked through their genealogies as class assignments. Along with the joys of revelation as lost relatives were discovered and hidden relationships were made plain, there was the universal feeling of sadness and loss as the students approached the time of slavery, when their genealogies became inextricably linked to chattel slavery. At that time, relationships have to be inferred from stories rather than being the subject of human documentation.

The need to consult property records to determine family history rather than the human records of births and deaths becomes a traumatic experience as the reality of what it means to be a slave hits hard on their consciousness. It is here that the word "muthufucka" becomes more than a word, and the rapetalistic context of black American history becomes oppressingly apparent as ancestors are reduced to names and values in property ledgers.

This trauma is similar to that experienced by victims of sexual assault and abuse. Feelings of shame are mixed with anger and denial as the students attempt to come to grips with the shame and humiliation of the rape of their mothers, the helplessness of their fathers, and the genuine character of this great American evil.

Besides leaving psychological pain, this realization of abandonment also has great significance for the healing of American racial wounds. How can whites expect blacks to feel wanted in America when most whites have denied the color in their own family trees? Most blacks in America have white relatives, but they have been systematically disowned of the social and economic benefits that should have resulted from these family arrangements. The plantation is the perfect model of the modern dysfunctional family in which the children, in this case, the black children, are blamed for the dysfunction of the family.

This is rejection at its most fundamental level. Do children who have been given up for adoption ever fully heal from the trauma of rejection? Blacks still feel this rejection as they attempt to gain social and economic parity after working without benefit of their social and economic inheritance for hundreds of years. The social costs of this rejection have been tremendous. The amnesia of white America has contributed to the racial gulf in this country. Most white Americans cannot understand this point because most whites came to America as part of the European migration of the late 1800s and early 1900s. For most whites, African Americans are simply another ethnic group that has not achieved the American dream through no fault of immigrant whites.

Most whites do not recognize the bitter interracial rivalry that existed between blacks and new immigrant white groups who were seeking to establish themselves on turf that was settled by black slavery. Although their parents were not involved in the slave trade, they were involved in joining other European immigrant groups who sought to solidify their own power at the expense of American blacks. The privilege of power has allowed this amnesia, which fails to acknowledge the continuing reality of racism and discrimination.

I do not believe that the scars from slavery and discrimination will be healed until the white community develops a realistic plan for black reparations. In keeping with the sexual abuse metaphor, the perpetrators must acknowledge their abusive status in order for genuine and long-lasting healing to occur. A four-hundred-year victimization that involves human sexuality, the most psychologically devastating of injuries, will not be easily healed. Any offense, from the Rodney King beating to the Mark Fuhrman testimony, can revive the memory of a centuries-old psychological trauma that America has yet to atone for in any meaningful manner.

This plan for reparations must come willingly from the white community. If it is forced, there always is the possibility of white backlash and resentment, as was seen during the Nixon and Reagan eras and now is manifest in sentiments against affirmative action. It must come willingly from the communities that directly and indirectly have benefited from black oppression. If white America cannot openly acknowledge its sins against the black community, then whites will continue to be the "muthufuckas" who have benefited from the sexual exploitation of their African American cousins.

In addition, I believe that black people tend to act like the victims of sexual assault and abuse. In this condition, posttraumatic stress and dysfunctional behavior are due to inability to integrate feelings of shame and powerlessness. I also believe that this underlying shame and a sense of resistance regarding sexual domination have led to the dominant sexual ethic in the black community, which I call the "ethic of discretion."

Sexual Ethic of Discretion

In reaction to these rapetalistic attitudes, African Americans have responded with silence regarding their sexual activities. Their sexual feelings were hidden and went underground, only to be expounded in sinful tunes and blues music that were not the parlance of everyday talk and discussion. This was done to protect black sexual life from prying and condemning European-American eyes. Although this ethic of discretion was a functional response to stereotyping and spying eyes, it meant that the most important area of human life was not going to receive the attention it required for the development of social life.

Sexual education, which traditionally had been the province of the family and elders, was limited by the ethic of discretion. Sexual discourse, which already was limited by European-American puritanical religious values, would undergo even greater repression as African Americans attempted to mimic their European-American cousins in their quest for middle-class status.

Spirituals represent a religious perspective that is passionate in its performance but not in its words. Discretion toward sexual matters is adhered to, but the performance is where bodily catharsis can take place. The religious ecstasy that accompanies the performance of spirituals involves body and soul. In the performance, pent-up sexual energy can be released and directed toward a divine presence that cares about both body and soul.

The sexually explicit language of sexual relationships is, of course, not proper for religious lyrics, but there is a distinctly sensual aspect to the performance of the spirituals. Their performance involves the deepest emotions that humans are capable of expressing. In the movement and moans and groans that accompany spirituals, one also can hear the beginnings of the sensuality of the blues.

Many elderly African women and men have told me about the relative silence they experienced concerning sexuality. It was thought that if children and adolescents did not know about sex, then they would be less likely to participate in illicit sexual activity. Sexual talk was relegated to the world of the blues, as "respectable" blacks were afraid to engage in open dialogue about such a troubling phenomenon.

Although this ethic of silence, was thought to be functional, like all ethics of reaction, it sorely lacked an ability to regulate behavior and promote healthy psychological attitudes. While European-Americans supposedly were having their neuroses healed by the sexual revelations generated through psychoanalysis, African Americans still were struggling with negative sexual stereotyping.

Evelyn Brooks Higginbotham, in her study of black Baptist churchwomen, discusses what I call the sexual ethics of discretion under the rubric of "the politics of respectability."[39] I disagree with Higginbotham's belief that this strategy was necessary and eventually politically liberating. Blacks were encouraged to be morally respectable as if their morality was worse than that of European-Americans. This idea that blacks must be moral in the eyes of whites is a strategy that places the African American community in a reactionary position. In this approach, blacks are forced to derive their ethics from standards and norms based on notions of white middle-class respectability. Not just black women advocated such an approach. Black leaders with such divergent viewpoints as Booker T. Washington and W. E. B. DuBois agreed that the black community deserved neither political nor social empowerment if it could not gain white respect by demonstrating that it conformed to the prevailing white middle-class social norms. A good example occurred in the Montgomery bus boycott, 1955–1956. A "morally respectable" black woman—Rosa Parks—had to be denied her seat on a bus before the black community could be mobilized to protest. Earlier, a young woman of lesser moral standing had been arrested, but she did not fit the prevailing moral criteria—or, in Higginbotham's terms, she was not morally "respectable" enough—and was not viewed as deserving her civil rights.

That many blacks bought into the need to develop a "respectable" family life in return for civil and human rights reveals the power of this complex of rapetalistic oppression on the psyches of whites and blacks alike. I am not suggesting that there is anything wrong with the desire for monogamous family stability. However, when it becomes the only ticket for entrance into American society, then it becomes a dangerous ideological check that white society has no intentions of honoring.

At the same time that the black middle class was constructing the image of the perfect black family, the black lower classes were developing the blues, ragtime, and swing—cultural styles that emphasized sexual freedom and bodily joy. The church eventually was forced to compromise with this blues ethic as the once-scorned gospel music became the musical modus operandi for black Christians. By this time, the middle-class church also had outlawed singing spirituals because they, too, were thought to represent a more direct expression of religious experience.

Psychologist Carl Jung, racist though he was, was correct in asserting that Europeans were projecting their negative views of sexuality onto the images of their black cousins.[46] We may ask whether Freudian notions of sexuality provided sexual healing for European-Americans or whether they simply were shifting their negative feelings about sexuality onto African bodies and sexuality. The movement of black bodies did not go unnoticed by white Americans and Europeans. The popularity of jazz, the conquering of Paris by the African-like dancing of Josephine Baker, and whites' imitation of black dancing styles show the deep levels of reciprocity that had developed between black and white cultures.

The spirituals held sway in the black community as the dominant mode of popular religious expression until the development of gospel music in the early twentieth century. Gospel music, which borrowed the syncopated beats of the blues and used them in sacred music, would replace spirituals as the most popular form of black sacred music, but it would continue to delve into the same issues of faith and feeling, family and freedom.

Faith and feeling were reconnected in the black church community by the music of the great gospel musicians before the black church could completely acquiesce to middle-class accommodationism. The black family's quest for freedom during the civil rights movement got its marching orders from the gospel music of Mahalia Jackson and the spirituals of the unknown bards of the black community. The style of Africa would continue to live for another generation as spirituals gave way to gospel music.

The Spirituals

An African Cultural Narrative Theology

Africana Narrative Theology and Cultural Context

The narrative of Nate Shaw revealed a continuation of the African-centered meanings that were present in African American spirituals. This Afro-Christian religious synthesis did not take place at the folk level until the Great and Second Awakenings, as the religious style of revivalist movements allowed the expression of feeling that signified contact with the divine world. This emotion-based religion was more appealing to Africans, whose religion featured heightened emotional states as a primary characteristic. Intense feeling bridged European and African religious styles. An outline of the development of African American Christianity would look like this.[1]

Historical Development of
African American Spirituals Theology

I. Sixteenth to mid-eighteenth century

African Religion ------- Rapetalistic Oppression --------- European Religion
    Narrativity   Doctrine
    Pluralism   Trinity
     Feeling   Catechism
    Possession
    Dance

In this period, African American religion is largely uninfluenced by European Christianity because of their different starting points for religious practice and beliefs. European religion stressed doctrines and literacy; African religion stressed experience and orality.

II. Mid-eighteenth century to mid-nineteenth century

African Religion ----------------- Revivalism ------------- European Religion
               Ritual process: dramas of salvation
                      Possession
                       Feeling
                       Dance
   led to African American religion—spirituals theology

The development of revivalism created a structural bridge that allowed Africans to integrate their own religious sensibilities into the framework of Christianity. American religion now placed enough emphasis on the experiential dimensions of religion that African Americans could develop a synthesis of these two religious perspectives. Some important features of African American religion are a moral perspective that recognized sin (but not original sin), an emphasis on family relationships, themes of freedom, and ideas of personal intimacy between God and nature.

The Political Dialectic

The autobiography of Nate Shaw is a powerful example of a narrative that is paradigmatic of the cultural and political dimensions of an African American spirituals theology. My analysis of this narrative revealed a complex dialectical relationship between the religious and the political aspects of black life. Nate Shaw's narrative confirmed my argument that the dialectical cultural-structural features of the African American spirituals have served as a model or classic religious paradigm for Africans in the United States. This model of spirituals allows us a method for interpreting the theology of African Americans in a way that is congruent with African American styles of meaning.

In the narrative of Nate Shaw, we saw how the religiously interpreted stories related to him by the members of his community, especially his grandmother, helped him gain an idea of the nature of freedom and justice. Shaw's capacities to care for his family and to think critically about the welfare of his community were developed and enhanced by the religious stories he heard in his community. These stories contributed to his eventual conversion experience, as he finally was able to see the connections his community made between individual spirituality and social protest.

In a burgeoning modern society in which little emphasis was placed on the importance of emotionality, African Americans combined their African ritual heritage with a budding evangelical Christian movement and developed a unique style of being religious that incorporated their political aspirations. Spirituals' structures of faith and feeling, family and freedom, intimacy between God and nature, and diversity have served as a narrative folk collection that informed the development of theology and ethics in the black community. This narrative form set the parameters for future black theological development.

Black religious thought and ethics may have taken a variety of paths, but they all have been linked to the spirituals' principles of meaning. Future African American thought and action were variations on these themes from spirituals, with spirituals acting as the deep metaphor that influenced thought and action. The idea that blacks are a "spiritual people" is given substance through recognition that they are the people who produced spirituals.

Black theology has suffered because its starting point for the interpretation of liberation often has been divorced from the narratives of black folk. Instead of listening to the people in the pews, black theologians have gravitated toward Eurocentric conceptions of freedom and justice.

Further analyses of other African American narratives that use the theology of spirituals as a touchstone would provide more detailed information about the cultural and political dialectical nature of African American religion. At the very least, this analysis based on spirituals, when utilized by black theologians, literary critics, and other scholars of African American religion and culture, would lead to more culturally appropriate interpretations. Spirituals as a guiding master metaphor, like the blues in the field of black literary criticism, would ground black theologians in an interpretive process derived from African American culture and values.

The application of various critical theories more reflective of Eurocentric concerns would be a second step of interpretation. The cultural-structural methodologies of DuBois and Hurston are examples of scholarship that is attuned both to the contours of black narration and to the concerns of academic theories of interpretation.

The Cultural Dialectic

Shaw's work was extremely important for the fields of African American history and culture because it gives scholars an idea of black folk meanings in a way that the study of movements and famous figures ill affords. The omission of ordinary people's experience from our written record deprives our historical self-image of much that is valuable. Historians who write about black Americans have been particularly guilty of this omission. George P. Rawkins, editor of a collection of slave narratives for the Federal Writer's Project, notes that the black person almost always has been portrayed as a victim "who never enters his own history as subject, but always as the object which abstract forces (have) fought."

The editor of *All God's Dangers* rejected the dehumanizing tendency which has limited our appreciation of what Eugene Genovese calls "the genius displayed by black people under the ultimate test of bondage." This book presents a figure unique in American autobiography and historical literature: an ordinary black man who speaks in his own voice and is both actor and interpreter of his own history.[2]

All God's Dangers successfully captures the ethos of African Americans. It is a spiritual ethos that reflects the cultural and political dialectical nature of African American religion and culture. Shaw's ability to relate the role and relevance of his family members and ancestors is important. He is like the African griot-storyteller who is responsible for the oral history of his people.

One of my claims is that the epistemological foundations of the black community are related to its African past. This African orientation—with its emphasis on family and the ancestors—is seen clearly in the autobiography of Nate Shaw. Perhaps the most poignant and revealing aspect of Shaw's narrative is found in the passages dealing with the relationships he formed with the younger prisoners. In this passage pertaining to Shaw's release from prison, we see Shaw reach the full level of spiritual maturity:

> I served my sentence out, didn't owe the state another day of my life. I had warned Vernon and his mother what day to come at me, and they come and got me. . . .
>
> I was in the room yet bathin when I heard Vernon come up the steps of that buildin—I knowed his footsteps, I didn't have to look and see it was him, I could hear him. He pushed the door open and I looked at his face. "Papa," he said, "Papa, it's time—"
>
> Quickly got ready; and my wife, when I walked out, she was settin there talkin with Mrs. Cook. Got in the car—them prisoner boys hated to see me leave, they hated it. Some of em called me "daddy," their daddy. There was a heap of em in there that never knowed their fathers; heap of em that never knowed their mothers.[3]

In prison, Shaw had created an extended family that paralleled and extended his own biological family. Not only was he "Papa" to his natural son, but also he was "daddy" to fatherless and motherless young men. The African concept of extended family was combined with a Christian sense of the family of God in a social situation plagued with family dissolution. The situation of rapetalistic oppression that devastated the black family was met by the ethos of the African American spirituals in which persons of religious maturity became spiritual fathers and mothers to those who need the nurture and guidance that only family can provide.

An Afrocentric narrative theology understands that the black community's responses to oppression have drawn from cultural strengths and structures that are related both to an African past and to their present evangelical Christian beliefs. This approach cannot be reduced either to the black community's reactions to oppression or to its adoption of Christian values. In fact, the black community has continued and adapted African cultural values and structures of meaning and applied them to their own situation.

In the case of Nate Shaw, we saw that this African American spirituals theological orientation provided Shaw with a deeper basis for actions that were based on the black community's religious ethos. It gave flesh to the ideas of justice and love that Shaw had heard all through his life as a member of a spiritual community.

> The possession theme in the Negro spiritual of North America seems a good deal closer to the vigorous dramatic concepts of the Africans. These songs do not describe a pale exercise. When the spirit captures an individual, according to the song, it is a memorable event. The spirit endows the individual with great powers; it transforms him physically and mentally. Expanding his whole role in life and death, the spirit gives the individual new strength, new direction, new motives and occupations, new capacity for wrestling with life, and above all a new sense of grandeur. The spirit sees to it that the natural world cooperates in all these new grand endeavors and performances.[4]

In the lives of African Americans, the political and the cultural are integrated into a worldview that has energized their struggle for personhood and human rights. In the case of Nate Shaw and many others like him, the ethos of spirituals provided an indigenous philosophical basis for the black community's political activism and social welfare. Black churches may not always have been willing or able to actualize the political dimensions of this dialectical philosophy, but the resources of the spirituals remain as resources for individual and social transformation.

The Psychological Dialectic

I have argued that a more thorough knowledge of West African notions of life and death will help us develop a keener understanding of the religious philosophy of African Americans. This slow acceptance reflects what I have termed the *psychological dialectic*. I have shown how historians and sociologists of African American religion have found similarities in the theological ideas of the African and African American peoples.

It is ironic that black theology is the last battlefield in the development of an Afrocentric black hermeneutic. These battles have been fought and won in the fields of linguistics, history, literary criticism, and family studies. The hesitant use of historical and social science information by black theologians has delayed this process. There has been an unfortunate dependence on a theological style that separates religion from history and philosophy from the social sciences.

Religion has played an important role for black people in their quest to gain acceptance in an American society that defined itself in exclusively Christian or Eurocentric terms. This situation, in which all things black and African were despised or, at best, ignored, has promoted a sense of African and African American cultural inferiority. The black community's own acceptance of this exclusivist and negative position meant that African American theology and philosophy would also define itself against its African past for reasons of doctrinal or philosophical purity. The narrative of Olaudah Equiano in the period of the Great Awakening, discussed in chapter 4, was an important digression from this almost uniform denigration of African culture by African Americans who had accepted evangelical Christianity. Blacks should not be faulted too heavily for consciously and unconsciously seeking protection from a racist society that already was convinced of the inferiority and "heathen" nature of black religion.

This denial or disgust with the African past, however, was not uniformly true, as I showed in the works of DuBois and Hurston. These early-twentieth-century scholars were willing to claim some sort of positive affinity with their African religious past. This affinity eventually may lead to a full-blown pan-African philosophy in which Africans and African Americans can celebrate their common traditions and beliefs without the need to compare them with Eurocentric ideas.

This ideological battle eventually must result in an Afrocentric black theology. The evidence for African style in black culture, religion, and philosophy by linguists, literary critics, historians, and social scientists is conclusive. It will be impossible to move to a more dialectical view of African American religion if black theologians continue to ignore or deprecate the presence of these Africanisms that have been the "signifying difference" in black religious life.[5]

An Africana Narrative Theology

This work points toward a narrative basis for theological reflection. African and evangelical Christian narratives had the power to create both theological and affective responses that helped African American individuals and communities to order their lives in theologically and socially responsible ways.

The theology of spirituals is a narrative theology that emphasizes human experience. It takes seriously the experiential dimension, in both its personal and social aspects, as the starting point for theological reflection. Joussa expresses this paradigm in this way:

> In this crisis situation I have chosen a starting-point that seems solid enough to me: the description and explanation of Christian experience, of the lived, commentated and interpreted experience of believers, of the fundamentals of faith in the state of radical accomplishment through experience itself . . . on condition, however, that this testimony is referred strictly to the origins of faith, and that it is approached critically, using all the resource of modernity.[6]

The use of hermeneutic procedures derived from the thick description of the narrative products and stories of religious persons is not dominant in contemporary theology. In the case of black theology, this issue is even more crucial in that African Americans rely more on narratives as their primary mode of theological expression and reflection. Black theologians seldom have had control over the ideological parameters of Christian theology and thus are even harder pressed to develop culturally appropriate modes of interpretation. Appropriate hermeneutic tools are of ultimate importance in an oppressed community's attempt to develop a sense of its own identity.[7]

The task for black theologians in the United States is similar to that for African theologians in Africa. Both must develop intellectually responsible theological positions that are responsive to both sides of the cultural dialectic: the African and the European. The worldview of the ancestors and Christian sensibility continue to provide many Africans in Africa and in the diaspora with their primary forms of discourse.

This religious discourse continues to be the roots from which African American culture grows. The political and cultural dialectical processes that led to the creation of the African American spirituals still are at work in the African American community. The cosmology of Africa continues to shape African American communal life. The spiritual is the African American classic among classics. It is the root from which modern narrative branches continue to grow. It influences the sort of person one becomes and provides the African American community with norms for behavior and belief.[8]

Every potter must have clay. The clay of African American religion can be found in the material of African culture, evangelical Christianity, and a social situation that fostered the development of a religious ethos unencumbered by social integration with the larger society. The angry and insistent themes of rap music, which reflect a situation in which more black men are in prison than in institutions of higher learning, continue the structural features of African music with appropriate political and cultural themes.

Black theologians must be able to listen and decode these messages as well, if black theology is to contribute to the struggle for black liberation. By basing the hermeneutic process in African American narration, the interpretive process will find itself in close proximity to the deepest meanings of the black community.

Postscript

At this point it may be illustrative to encounter another offering in Eliade's journal about African American religion:

We could hear a radio turned up uncommonly loud, amplified to a din. Modern American music, jazz, Negro spirituals, love songs. Suddenly, we both started: we seemed to recognize the melody. It was exactly like one we had heard in January 1957 at the Church of Deliverance, the church of a black sect in Chicago. Cornelius Bolle had taken us. A room as huge as a concert hall. On the platform, four pianos and a choir of several hundred men and women, all dressed in green and white. The pianos accentuated the jazz like quality yet without managing to lessen the heart-rending melancholy, the nameless despair which breathed from that haunting melody. The refrain stood out: "Jesus, Jesus!" At one point one of the female choristers fainted. We had noticed her when her arms began to move like two broken wings. Afterward, they carried her outside. I shall always remember the two black women seated behind us, extraordinarily beautiful, distinguished, soberly and yet so elegantly dressed.[1]

Archie Smith Jr., the African American theologian and ethicist, when pressed to describe the essence of African American ethics, likened it to modern jazz, with its emphasis on improvisation and flexibility. The jazz metaphor of Smith, the "signifyin' " metaphor of Gates, and Baker's blues metaphor all represent attempts by African American scholars to provide appropriate metaphoric designations for the core features of African American religion and culture.[2]

I have argued that the metaphor of the spiritual should have priority for historical and cultural reasons, for it was in the creation of the spirituals that African Americans first developed their theological and cultural orientation. The spirituals were the first body of black narration by which African Americans captured the essence of their African heritage as well as the expression of their new evangelical Christian perspective.

In sum, the spirituals can serve as an Afrocentric narrative hermeneutic for black theology and cultural criticism, just as they inspired generations of African Americans to continue their struggle in a New World. African Americans may be a long way from home, but they brought a part of Africa with them when they came. They transformed evangelical Christian religion into spirituals that carried forth the best in both traditions. Spirituals now can serve to carry us further into more faithful interpretations of African American religion and culture.

This work, in part, is an attempt to break the theoretical logjam confronting black critical theory, much of which has been due to the controversy over the validity of Afrocentric criticism. I hope that I have shown how the recognition of African cultural structures has been important in the development of black critical theory since the work of DuBois early in this century. The idea that African Americans employ African structures of meaning was implicit in his work and in the work of scholars such as Hurston and Herskovits. The denial of this African relationship has had more to do with the politics of knowledge than with the evidence of empirical data.

African Americans' hope for acceptance by the American status quo has led many scholars and black leaders to deny this African past in order to downplay non–European-American aspects of black cultural life. Arguments for and against Afrocentricity often are as much arguments for and against the state of black acceptance into the American mainstream. Those who have little faith in America's willingness to accept African Americans on equal terms as the descendants of Africa tend to stress the African nature of black life. Those who hope for American acceptance of blacks into the mainstream of cultural and political life attempt to decrease the Otherness of blacks and thereby shrink the cultural differences.

The position I have stated insists on the reality of the African presence in African American cultural life. This presence should be acknowledged with an understanding that cultural differences do not mean inferiority, shame, or antipathy. In fact, if different cultural structures can be unashamedly acknowledged without fear and loathing, then perhaps there still is hope for the Bosnias and South Central LAs of our time.

Differences do exist between cultural groups. They exist because of the particularities of social location and historical circumstance. They exist as positive expressions of culture and as cultural reactions to oppressive conditions. The scholar's task is to recognize the cultural differences between groups and to help us to understand the intercultural and intracultural factors that have shaped those differences.

The truth is the light, and this quest for truth motivates us in our search for knowledge. The truth of cultures, however, is not static. As African Americans continue to interact, grow, and develop, their cultural traits also will change, but I believe that these cultural structures will continue to be influenced by its classic expression, spirituals.

This cultural form embodies in its verses and rhythms the hard-earned legacy and meanings of a proud African people who "made a way out of no way" and with their collective imagination created a cultural form witnesses to the desire for faith and feeling, family and freedom. These simple and obvious things were the most desired by a people who chose to sing and create in hope of a better day. This work is an homage to the spirit of these ancestors who still yearn to see their children attain these most basic—but most important—of life's treasures.

> He is King of kings,
> He is Lord of lords,
> Jesus Christ, the first and the last,
> No man works like Him.

> He built a platform in the air,
> He meets the saints from everywhere;
> He pitched a tent on Canaan's ground,

And broke the Roman kingdom down;
I know that my Redeemer lives,
And by his death sweet blessings gives.

He is King of kings,
He is Lord of lords,
Jesus Christ, the first and the last,
No man works like Him.

Notes

CHAPTER I

1. John G. Jackson, *Introduction to African Civilizations* (New York: University Books, 1970).

2. T. S. Eliot, "The Dry Salvages," in *The Four Quartets* (San Diego: Harvest/ HBJ, 1971), p. 39. The passage includes these words: "Time the destroyer is time the preserver/Like the river with its cargo of dead negroes, cows and chicken coops."

3. James Baldwin, *The Evidence of Things Not Seen* (New York: Holt, Rinehart and Winston, 1985), p. 83.

4. Donald G. Mathews, *Religion in the Old South* (Chicago: University of Chicago Press, 1975); Mechal Sobel, *Trabelin' On: The Slave Journey to an Afro-Baptist Faith* (1979; Princeton: Princeton University Press, 1988).

5. Gayraud S. Wilmore, *Black Religion and Black Radicalism: An Interpretation of the Religious History of Afro-American People,* 2d ed. (Maryknoll, N.Y.: Orbis, 1983), p. 237.

6. Benjamin E. Mays, *The Negro's God as Reflected in His Literature* (1938; New York: Atheneum, 1968), pp. 19–30; Martin Luther King Jr., *Stride toward Freedom: The Montgomery Story* (New York: Harper & Brothers, 1958).

7. Mays, *The Negro's God,* p. 29. This "subtle" approach recently has been discussed under the rubric of "signifyin' " in African American discourse: a process that involves the use of hidden meanings and other forms of linguistic and bodily expression that relate meaning through metaphorical and metonymical processes of speech.

8. Geneva Smitherman, *Talkin and Testifyin: The Language of Black America* (Boston: Houghton Mifflin, 1977), discusses this phenomenon in verbal narrative, while Henry Louis Gates Jr., *The Signifying Monkey: A Theory of African-American*

Literary Criticism (New York: Oxford University Press, 1988), discusses this process in the development of black literature.

9. Miles Mark Fisher, *Negro Slave Songs in the United States* (New York: Citadel, 1953).

10. Raymond Williams, *Marxism and Literature* (New York: Oxford University Press, 1977).

11. Joseph R. Washington Jr., *Black Sects and Cults* (Garden City, N.Y.: Anchor/Doubleday, 1973), pp. 73–74, 91. See also pp. 89–91.

12. Mathews, *Religion in the Old South*, and Milton C. Sernett, *Black Religion and American Evangelicalism: White Protestants, Plantation Missions, and the Flowering of Negro Christianity, 1787–1865* (Metuchen, N.J.: Scarecrow Press, 1975), have demonstrated quite ably the African and evangelical Christian roots of African American religion. See also Albert J. Raboteau, *Slave Religion: The "Invisible Institution" in the Antebellum South* (New York: Oxford University Press, 1978).

13. Raboteau, *Slave Religion*, pp. 48–55.

14. Ibid., p. 74.

15. Ibid.

16. Ibid., p. 250.

17. Erika Bourguignon, "Ritual Dissociation and Possession Belief in Caribbean Negro Religion," in *Afro-American Anthropology*, ed. Norman E. Whitten and John F. Szwed, (N.Y.: Free Press, 1970), p. 88; quoted by Raboteau, *Slave Religion*, p. 63.

18. Raboteau, *Slave Religion*, p. 63.

19. John S. Mbiti, *African Religions and Philosophy*, 2d ed. (Oxford: Heinemann, 1989), is representative of the African theology movement that challenged this dualistic thinking on the African continent.

20. Sheila S. Walker, *Ceremonial Spirit Possession in Africa and Afro-America* (Leiden: E. J. Brill, 1972). Margaret Fields, "Spirit Possession in Ghana," in, *Spirit Mediumship and Society in Africa,* ed. John Beattie and John Middleton (New York: Africana, 1969).

21. Raboteau, *Slave Religion,* p. 74.

22. Roland Barthes, *Mythologies* (New York: Noonday Press, 1957), pp. 121, 122.

23. Stephen Hawking, *A Brief History of Time: From the Big Bang to Black Holes* (New York: Bantam, 1988), pp. 56, 187.

24. Eugene D. Genovese, *Roll, Jordan, Roll: The World the Slaves Made* (New York: Pantheon, 1974), pp. 210–213.

25. Ibid., p. 213.

26. Ibid., p. 249.

27. Ibid., pp. 210–213.

28. Ibid., pp. 217–219. Sobel, *Trabelin' On*, is quite instructive of the process of African religious transmission to African Americans.

29. Genovese, *Roll, Jordan, Roll*, p. 213.

30. Lawrence W. Levine, *Black Culture and Black Consciousness: Afro-American Folk Thought from Slavery to Freedom* (New York: Oxford University Press, 1977), p. 33.

31. Ibid., p. 35.

32. Ibid., p. 39.

33. The back to Africa movement has been a consistent theme in African American religion, from the ideology of Blyden and Turner in the nineteenth century to the contemporary ideology of Rastafarianism. A good introduction to the religious significance of these movements is found in Gayraud Wilmore, *Black Religion and Black Radicalism*.

34. John Lovell Jr., *Black Song: The Forge and the Flame: How the Afro-American Spiritual Was Hammered Out* (New York: Macmillan, 1972).

35. Howard Thurman, *Deep River and the Negro Spiritual Speaks of Life and Death* (Richmond, Ind.: Friends United Press, 1975).

36. John J. Ansbro, *Martin Luther King Jr.: The Making of a Mind* (Maryknoll, N.Y.: Orbis, 1982); Stephen B. Oates, *Let the Trumpet Sound: The Life of Martin Luther King Jr.* (New York: Mentor, 1982).

37. Wole Soyinka, *Art, Dialogue and Outrage: Essays on Literature and Culture* (1988; New York: Pantheon, 1993); *Myth, Literature, and the African World* (New York: Cambridge University Press, 1976); Ketu Datrak, *Wole Soyinka and Modern Tragedy: A Study of Dramatic Theory and Practice* (Westport, Conn.: Greenwood Press, 1986); and Obi Maduakor, *Wole Soyinka: An Introduction to His Writings* (New York: Garland, 1986).

CHAPTER 2

1. Charles H. Long, *Significations: Signs, Symbols, and Images in the Interpretation of Religion* (Philadelphia: Fortress Press, 1986), pp. 175–176.

2. Theophus H. Smith, *Conjuring Culture: Biblical Formations of Black America* (New York: Oxford University Press, 1994), p. 122.

3. Jahn Jahnheinz, *Muntu: The New African Culture* (New York: Grove Press, 1961), p. 220.

4. William Andrews, *Sisters of the Spirit* (Bloomington: Indiana University Press, 1986).

5. Lovell, *Black Song: The Forge and the Flame*, pp. 354–355.

6. W. E. B. DuBois, *The Souls of Black Folk* (1903; reprint, New York: Bantam, 1989), pp. 182–183.

7. Hans Dieter Dretzel, "On the Political Meaning of Culture," in *Beyond the Crisis*, ed. Norman Birnbaum (New York: Oxford University Press, 1977), p. 84.

8. Nancy Boyd-Franklin, *Black Families in Therapy: A Multisystems Approach* (New York: Guilford Press, 1989), p. 78.

9. T. S. Eliot, "The Dry Salvages," in *Four Quartets*, p. 40.

10. Olaudah Equiano, "The Life of Olaudah Equiano," in *The Classic Slave Narratives*, ed. Henry Louis Gates Jr. (New York: Mentor Books, 1987), p. 22.

11. Ibid., p. 24.

12. Fisher, *Negro Slave Songs in the United States*. See also John Lovell's treatment of this issue in his *Black Song: The Forge and the Flame*, p. 112.

13. Sterling Stuckey, *The Ideological Origins of Black Nationalism* (Boston: Beacon Press, 1972).

14. Mathews, *Religion in the Old South*, Sobel, *Trabelin' On*; and several other historians will be drawn on throughout the course of this work to demonstrate the relationship between African and African American religion.

15. Smitherman, *Talkin and Testifyin*; and Herbert Gutman, *The Black Family in Slavery and Freedom, 1750–1920* (New York: Pantheon, 1976) are two of the leading voices in linguistic and family studies who have shown convincingly the interrelatedness of African and African American culture.

16. Winthrop Jordan, *White over Black: American Attitudes toward the Negro, 1550–1812* (Chapel Hill: University of North Carolina Press, 1968), pp. 439–440.

17. Dick Hebdige, *Subculture: The Meaning of Style* (New York: Metheun, 1979); Williams, *Marxism and Literature*; Jean Comaroff, *Body of Power, Spirit of Resistance: The Culture and History of a South African People* (Chicago: University of Chicago Press, 1985). These texts represent a methodological approach that calls for close attention to the production of new cultural orientations through historical dialectical processes.

18. Paul Ricoeur, "Dialogue with Paul Ricoeur," in *Dialogues with Contemporary Continental Thinkers: The Phenomenological Heritage*, ed. Richard Kearney (Manchester: Manchester University Press, 1984), pp. 17, 26–27.

19. Smitherman, *Talkin and Testifyin*, p. 76.

20. Ricoeur, "Dialogue with Paul Rocoeur," pp. 42–43.

21. Mary Frances Berry and John W. Blassingame, "Africa, Slavery and the Roots of Contemporary Black Culture," in *Chant of Saints: A Gathering of Afro-American Literature, Art, and Scholarship*, ed. Michael S. Harper and Robert B. Stepto (Urbana: University of Illinois Press, 1979), p. 256.

22. By "classic," I mean a work of art that has stood the test of time and has developed into a universally recognized work of excellence within a particular community. A religious classic is a work which draws us into an awareness of sacred truth that is inherently dialectical in its manifestation and proclamation of a sacred reality. See David Tracy, *Analogical Imagination: Christian Theology and the Culture of Pluralism* (New York: Crossroad, 1981), pp. 216–218.

23. Williams, *Marxism and Literature*, pp. 128–135, refers to "structures of feelings" in his analysis of the ways in which culture embodies the hopes, wishes, and desires of particular social groups.

24. James W. Fernandez, *Persuasions and Performances: The Play of Tropes in Culture* (Bloomington: Indiana University Press, 1986), pp. 30–62.

25. James W. Fernandez, *Bwiti: An Ethnography of the Religious Imagination in Africa* (Princeton: Princeton University Press, 1982).

26. Fernandez explains his narrative method, which involves a discovery and interaction of metaphors in cultural life, in *Persuasions and Performances*. Hayden White also develops a metaphoric perspective for historical analysis in *Tropics of Discourse: Essays in Cultural Criticism* (Baltimore: Johns Hopkins University Press, 1978) and *Metahistory: The Historical Imagination in Nineteenth-Century Europe* (Baltimore: Johns Hopkins University Press, 1973).

27. The work of Michael Goldberg, *Theology and Narrative: A Critical Introduction* (Nashville: Abingdon Press, 1982), is a helpful introduction into the realm

of methodology in narrative theology. Goldberg examines the narrative methodologies of several contemporary theologians.

28. H. Richard Niebuhr, *The Meaning of Revelation* (New York: Macmillan, 1941) and *The Responsible Self: An Essay in Christian Moral Philosophy* (New York: Harper & Row, 1963). Niebuhr's perspective has found acceptance by several African American theologians, notably James H. Cone in *God of the Oppressed* (New York: Seabury Press, 1975) and Archie Smith Jr. in *The Relational Self: Ethics and Therapy from a Black Church Perspective* (Nashville: Abingdon Press, 1982).

29. Niebuhr, *The Responsible Self*, p. 157; and David Tracy, *Blessed Rage for Order: The New Pluralism in Theology* (New York: Seabury Press, 1975).

30. James McClendon, *Biography as Theology: How Life Stories Can Remake Today's Theology* (Nashville: Abingdon Press, 1974) and Stanley Hauerwas, *Truthfulness and Tragedy: Further Investigations into Christian Theological Ethics* (South Bend, Ind.: University of Notre Dame Press, 1977).

31. Fitz John Porter Poole, "Metaphors and Maps: Towards Comparison in the Anthropology of Religion," *Journal of the American Academy of Religion* 54 (Autumn 1986): 411–457.

32. A useful analysis of contemporary narrative theologians is provided by Gary Comstock in "Two Types of Narrative Theology," *Journal of the American Academy of Religion* 55 (Winter 1987): 687–717. Comstock divided narrative theologians into two camps: One emphasizes the absolute "truth" of the Christian revelation, the "Yale" group, and another, the "Chicago School," emphasizes the historical and sociological context in the hermeneutic enterprise.

33. Niebuhr, *The Responsible Self*, p. 158.

34. Robert J. Schreiter, *Constructing Local Theologies* (Maryknoll, N.Y.: Orbis Books, 1985), is a stimulating methodological defense for the utilization of religious materials that are indigenous to a particular people in the development of theological formulations.

35. Theodore Rosengarten, *All God's Dangers: The Life of Nate Shaw* (New York: Avon Books, published by arrangement with Alfred A. Knopf, 1974).

36. Long, *Significations*; Cone, *God of the Oppressed*.

37. Genovese, *Roll, Jordan, Roll*; and Levine, *Black Culture and Black Consciousness*, employ a dialectical method that attends to the structures and themes of African American Christianity.

38. DuBois, *The Souls of Black Folk*, p. 178.

39. Ibid., p. 3.

CHAPTER 3

1. Mircea Eliade, *No Souvenirs: Journal, 1957–1969* (New York: Harper & Row, 1977), p. 206.

2. Newbell Niles Puckett, *Folk Beliefs of the Southern Negro* (1926; reprint, Montclair, N.J.: Patterson Smith, 1968). This work, first published in 1926, sets the stage for the denigration of the African characteristics in African American religious behavior and thought. See also E. Franklin Frazier, *The Negro Church in America*

(New York: Schocken Books, 1964). Frazier was the leading African American sociologist of his day. He was a staunch opponent of the presence of meaningful African survivals in Negro religion, although he mentions several instances of African-influenced religious behavior. Washington, *Black Sects and Cults*, continued this view of African American religion.

3. John W. Blassingame, *The Slave Community: Plantation Life in the Antebellum South* (New York: Oxford University Press, 1972). Blassingame was one of the first historians who turned to the slave narratives as primary resources for the interpretation of African American life. V. P. Franklin, *Black Self-Determination: A Cultural History of the Faith of the Fathers* (Westport, Conn.: Lawrence Hill, 1984), is a recent attempt to utilize the slave narratives to inform an interpretation of African American culture.

4. Juan Luis Segundo, *The Liberation of Theology* (Maryknoll, N.Y.: Orbis Books, 1976). Segundo provides an excellent discussion of the need for adequate sociological and historical information for theological purposes. This concern has not gone totally unrepresented in American and European political theology. H. R. Niebuhr, *The Responsible Self*, and Paul Tillich, *Theology of Culture* (London: Oxford University Press, 1959), also were concerned with the relationship of culture to theological reflection.

5. Equiano, "The Life of Olaudah Equiano."

6. Wilmore, *Black Religion and Black Radicalism,* first published in 1972, is in part a history of this defensive stance of the black church. Hebdige, *Subculture: The Meaning of Style;* and Comaroff, *Body of Power, Spirit of Resistance,* seek to develop and understanding of cultural resistance through social practice.

7. Iain MacRobert, *The Black Roots and White Racism of Early Pentecostalism in the U.S.A.* (New York: St. Martin's Press, 1988). Wyatt T. Walker, *"Somebody's Calling My Name": Black Sacred Music and Social Change* (Valley Forge, Pa.: Judson Press, 1979), presents a history of black Christian music in which he demonstrates its interaction with American culture.

8. MacRobert, *The Black Roots and White Racism of Early Pentecostalism in the U.S.A.,* presents pentecostalism as an African cultural form that served as a form of resistance to American racism at cultural and religious levels.

9. Ibid., pp. 89–90.

10. Reinhold Niebuhr, *The Nature and Destiny of Man: A Christian Interpretation,* 2 vols. (New York: Charles Scribner's Sons, 1941–1943); Paul Tillich, *Systematic Theology,* 3 vols. (Chicago: University of Chicago Press, 1951–1963).

11. In anthropology, James W. Fernandez in *Bwiti* and in *Persuasions and Performances* stresses the central role of metaphor in the construction of meaning. In theology, Sallie McFague in *Metaphorical Theology: Models of God in Religious Language* (Philadelphia: Fortress Press, 1982), emphasizes the central place of metaphors in the construction of Christian theology.

12. DuBois, *The Souls of Black Folk,* p. 178.

13. Ibid., pp. 134–135.

14. Ibid., p. 134.

15. Ibid., pp. 135–136.

16. Ibid., p. 134.

17. Ibid., p. 135.

18. Ibid.

19. Ibid.

20. Ibid., p. 181.

21. Ibid., pp. 186–187.

22. Ibid., p. 139.

23. Zora Neale Hurston, *The Sanctified Church* (Berkeley: Turtle Island, 1983), p. 79.

24. Ibid., p. 80.

25. Ibid.

26. Ibid.

27. Ibid., pp. 103–104.

28. Melville J. Herskovits, *The Myth of the Negro Past* (Boston: Beacon, 1969), pp. 269–270; Robert Farris Thompson, *Flash of the Spirit: African and Afro-American Art and Philosophy* (New York: Random House, 1983), p. 1; and Noel King, *Religions of Africa* (New York: Harper & Row, 1970), p. 23.

29. Robert Hemenway, *Zora Neale Hurston: A Literary Biography* (Urbana: University of Illinois Press, 1977).

30. Herskovits, *The Myth of the Negro Past*, p. 265.

31. Victor Turner, *The Drums of Affliction: A Study of Religious Processes among the Ndembu of Zambia* (Oxford: Clarendon Press, 1968), pp. 89–127; *Dramas, Fields, and Metaphors: Symbolic Action in Human Society* (Ithaca: Cornell University Press, 1974); and *The Ritual Process: Structure and Anti-Structure* (Ithaca: Cornell University Press, 1969). Turner's work is classic in anthropological structural analysis, using the rubrics of communitas and liminality.

32. Comaroff, *Body of Power, Spirit of Resistance*, p. 259, and Turner, *The Ritual Process*, pp. 106, 145.

33. Zora Neale Hurston, *Mules and Men* (Bloomington: Indiana University Press, 1935), pp. 191–291.

34. Herbert Aptheker, ed., *The Correspondence of W. E. B. DuBois: Selections, 1877–1934*, vol. 1 (Amherst: University of Massachusetts Press, 1973), pp. 106–107.

35. Frank Parkin, *Max Weber* (London: Tavistock, 1982), pp. 29–30.

36. Franz Boas, *Race, Language and Culture* (New York: Macmillan, 1940).

37. Fernandez, *Bwiti*.

38. Aptheker, ed., *The Correspondence of W.E.B. DuBois*, p. 346, and Hemenway, *Zora Neale Hurston*, pp. 37–39 and 347–355; Arnold Rampersand, *The Art and Imagination of W. E. B. DuBois*, 2d ed. (New York: Schocken Books, 1990).

39. I. Hassan, "The Culture of Postmodernism," *Theory, Culture and Society* 2 (1985): 119–132.

40. Stephen E. Toulmin, *Cosmopolis: The Hidden Agenda of Modernity* (New York: Free Press, 1990).

41. Walter Ong, *Orality and Literacy: The Technologizing of the Word* (New York: Routledge, 1982).

42. C. Eric Lincoln and Lawrence H. Mamiya, *The Black Church in the African American Experience* (Durham: Duke University Press, 1990). See especially chapter 4, "The Black Pentecostals: The Spiritual Legacy with a Black Beginning," pp. 76–91.

43. Evelyn Brooks Higginbotham, *Righteous Discontent: The Women's Movement in the Black Baptist Church, 1880–1920* (Cambridge: Harvard University Press, 1993), pp. 120–149.

44. See, for example, Andrews, *Sisters of the Spirit.*

45. David Roberts, "Out of Africa: the superb artwork of ancient Nubia," *Smithsonian Magazine* 24 (June 1993): 99–100.

46. Ishmael Reed, *Mumbo Jumbo* (Garden City, N.Y.: Doubleday, 1972).

CHAPTER 4

1. Houston A. Baker Jr., *The Journey Back: Issues in Black Literature and Criticism* (Chicago: University of Chicago Press, 1980), p. 135.

2. Stephen Henderson, *Understanding the New Black Poetry: Black Speech and Black Music as Poetic References* (New York: Morrow, 1973).

3. Ibid., p. 7.

4. Ibid., pp. 11–66.

5. Ibid., pp. 42–43.

6. Ibid., p. 21.

7. Baker, *The Journey Back*, p. 165.

8. Ibid., p. xiv.

9. Ibid., p. xvii.

10. Houston A. Baker Jr., *Blues, Ideology and Afro-American Literature: A Vernacular Theory* (Chicago: University of Chicago Press, 1984).

11. Ibid., pp. 31–50.

12. Ibid., p. 1.

13. Ibid., pp. 3–4.

14. Houston A. Baker, Jr., "Belief, Theory, and Blues: Notes for a Post-Structuralist Criticism of Afro-American Literature," in *Studies in Black American Literature*, vol. 2, ed. Joe Weixlmann and Chester J. Fontenot (Greenwood, Fla.: Penkevill, 1986), p. 9.

15. Ibid., p. 11.

16. Ibid., p. 2.

17. Ibid., p. 5.

18. James Boggs, *Revolution and Evolution in the Twentieth Century* (New York: Monthly Review Press, 1974), is one example of black Marxist interpretation.

19. Craig Werner, "New Democratic Vistas: Toward a Pluralistic Genealogy," in *Studies in Black American Literature*, vol. 2, ed. Joe Weixlmann and Chester J. Fontenot (Greenwood, Fla.: Penekevill, 1986), p. 79.

20. Baker, "Belief, Theory, and Blues," p. 5.

21. Baker, *Blues, Ideology and Afro-American Literature*, pp. 21–50.

22. Ibid., p. 37.

23. Equiano, "The Life of Olaudah Equiano," p. 100.

24. Baker, *Blues, Ideology and Afro-American Literature*, pp. 32–33.

25. Equiano, "The Life of Olaudah Equiano," pp. 13–14.

26. Equiano writes in the eighteenth century. This positive view of African religion was to undergo a negative trend in the nineteenth century as American black leaders began to accept the negative view of "pagan" African religious beliefs. See "E. W. Blyden's Legacy and Questions," in V. Y. Mudimbe, *The Invention of Africa: Gnosis, Philosophy, and the Order of Knowledge* (Bloomington: Indiana University Press, 1988), pp. 98–134; and Anthony Appiah, "Alexander Crummell and the Invention of Africa," *Massachusetts Review* 31 (1990): 385–406.

27. Smitherman, *Talkin and Testifyin,* p. 82. "Signification" refers to the act of talking negatively about somebody through stunning and clever verbal put-downs. In the black vernacular, it is more commonly referred to as "sigging" or "signifyin'." More will be said about this concept of signification when we examine the black literary theory of Henry Louis Gates Jr.

28. Baker, *Blues, Ideology and Afro-American Literature*, p. 47.

29. Ibid., pp. 47–48.

30. Ibid., p. 49.

31. Frederick Douglass, *Life and Times of Frederick Douglass: Written by Himself* (1881; Secaucus, N.J.: Citadel Press, 1983), p. 341.

32. Linda Brent, "Incidents in the Life of a Slave Girl," in *The Classic Slave Narratives*, ed. Henry Louis Gates Jr. (New York: Mentor Books, 1987), p. 509.

33. Ibid., p. 510.

34. Ibid., p. 512.

35. Ibid., pp. 326–331.

36. Baker, *Blues, Ideology and Afro-American Literature*, pp. 54–55.

37. Ibid., pp. 50–56. This passage contains Baker's analysis of the effect of gender in Brent's writing. In his analysis, even the sexual victimization of black women is superseded by the category of economics. "This system granted such bizarre power to white males that it might well have been designated an 'economics of rape' " (p. 55). In my comments about the social context, I will argue that sexual violence, economic oppression, and racism should be viewed as an interrelated phenomenon, which I call "rapetalistic oppression." In this view, any of these phenomena may take the fore, but the other two will be contributing to its power.

38. Ibid., pp. 81–87.

39. Baker, *The Journey Back*, p. 15.

40. Ibid., pp. 36–37.

41. Ibid., pp. 10, 41.

42. Henry Louis Gates Jr., " 'Race,' Writing and Difference," first appeared as an edited volume of essays comprising an issue of *Critical Inquiry* 12 (Autumn 1985). I will be referring to this journal in this work. In *Black Literature and Literary Theory* (New York: Metheun, 1984), Gates was the author of "Criticism in the Jungle" and "The Blackness of Blackness: A Critique of the Sign and the Signifying Monkey." Gates's editor's introduction is entitled "Writing 'Race' and the Difference it Makes." He also is the author of *Figures in Black: Words, Signs and the*

"Racial" Self (New York: Oxford University Press, 1987) and *The Signifying Monkey: A Theory of African-American Literary Criticism.* (New York: Oxford University University Press, 1988). These are Gates's most comprehensive attempts at both explaining and applying his theory.

43. Gates, " 'Race,' Writing and Difference," pp. 13, 15.

44. Gates, "Criticism in the Jungle," in *Black Literature and Literary Theory*, p. 8, and "The Blackness of Blackness: A Critique of the Sign and the Signifying Monkey," pp. 285–321. See pp. 285–291 for Gates's definition of "signifyin'."

45. Gates, *The Signifying Monkey*, pp. 3–51.

46. Gates, "The blackness of blackness," in *Black Literature and Literary Theory*, p. 286.

47. Gates, *The Signifying Monkey*, p. 21.

48. Ibid., pp. xxv–xxvi.

49. A most perceptive understanding of this defect in their critical efforts is rendered by Elaine Showalter in "A Criticism of Our Own: Autonomy and Assimilation in Afro-American and Feminist Literary Theory," in *The Future of Literary Theory*, ed. Ralph Cohen (New York: Routledge, 1989), pp. 347–369.

50. Dexter Fisher and Robert B. Stepto, eds., *Afro-American Literature: The Reconstruction of Instruction* (New York: Modern Language Association of America, 1979), pp. 44–68.

51. Gates, *Figures in Black*, pp. 175–176.

52. Ibid., p. 190.

53. Ibid., pp. 161–163.

54. This criticism has been made most cogently by Joyce A. Joyce, "The Black Canon: Reconstructing Black American Literary Criticism," *New Literary History* 18 (Winter 1987): 335–344.

CHAPTER 5

1. King, *Stride toward Freedom*, pp. 134–135.

2. Ibid., pp. 135–138.

3. Deborah Gray White, *Ar'n't I a Woman? Female Slaves in the Plantation South* (New York: Norton, 1985), p. 33.

4. Angela Davis, *Women, Race and Class* (New York: Random House, 1981), and White, *Ar'n't I a Woman?* are two good sources.

5. Collections of the music of Southern African American communities reveal these family themes. Two good sources are Nicholas George Julius Ballanta-(Taylor), *Saint Helena Island Spirituals* (New York: Institute of Musical Art, 1924); and Lydia Parrish, *Slave Songs of the Georgia Sea Islands* (1942; Athens: University of Georgia Press, 1992). John Lovell Jr., in the most thorough work about the spiritual, also makes this and many other excellent points concerning the African American spiritual in *Black Song: The Forge and the Flame*, pp. 274–281.

6. A. Philip Randolph, "Lynching: Capitalism Its Cause; Socialism Its Cure," *The Messenger* (March 1919), as quoted in August Meier, Elliott Rudwick, and Fran-

cis L. Broderick, eds., *Black Protest Thought in the Twentieth Century*, 2d ed. (Indianapolis: Bobbs-Merrill, 1971), pp. 87–88.

7. Ibid., pp. 89–90.

8. Rosengarten, *All God's Dangers*, was awarded the National Book Award in the area of current events and is used extensively by scholars in the fields of African American, Southern, and labor history.

9. H. J. Geiger, "Review of *All God's Dangers: The Life of Nate Shaw*," by Theodore Rosengarten," *The New Republic* 171 (October 12, 1974): 24.

10. Rosengarten, *All God's Dangers*, p. 468.

11. Ibid., p. 10.

12. Ibid., p. 7.

13. Ibid., p. 27.

14. Ibid., p. 25.

15. Ibid., p. 400.

16. Ibid., p. 401.

17. Ibid., p. 9.

18. Ibid., p. 27.

19. Ibid., p. 14.

20. Ibid., p. 7.

21. Ibid., p. 476.

22. Ibid., p. 351.

23. Ibid.

24. Preston N. Williams, "The Ethics of Power," in *Quest for a Black Theology*, ed. James J. Gardner and J. Deotis Roberts (Philadelphia: Pilgrim Press, 1971), pp. 82–96. In this provocative and seminal article, Williams begins to develop a theological ethics of "soul."

25. Toni Morrison, *The Bluest Eye* (New York: Holt, Rinehart and Winston, 1970).

26. Toni Morrison, *Sula* (New York: Alfred A. Knopf, 1974).

27. Toni Morrison, *Tar Baby* (New York: Alfred A. Knopf, 1981).

28. Toni Morrison, *Song of Solomon* (New York: Alfred A. Knopf, 1977).

29. Toni Morrison, *Beloved* (New York: Alfred A. Knopf, 1987).

30. Chinua Achebe, *Things Fall Apart* (New York: McDowell, Obolensky, 1959).

31. Morrison, *Beloved*, p. 108.

32. David Bradley, *The Chaneysville Incident* (New York: Avon Books, 1981).

33. Morrison, *Beloved*, p. 23.

34. Ibid.

35. "Memoirs of Old Elizabeth, a Coloured Woman" (1863), in *Six Women's Slave Narratives* ed. Henry Louis Gates Jr., (New York: Oxford University Press), pp. 3–4.

36. Federal Writers' Project, *Lay My Burden Down* (Chicago: University of Chicago Press, 1945), p. 164.

37. Ibid., pp. 165–166.

38. Ibid., p. 174.

39. Higginbotham, *Righteous Discontent*, pp. 185–229.

40. Carl Gustav Jung, *Modern Man in Search of a Soul* (New York: Harcourt, Brace, 1933).

CHAPTER 6

1. Molefi Asanti, in *The Afrocentric Idea* (Philadelphia: Temple University Press, 1981), uses the term *Afrocentricity* to designate what I have been doing in this work, namely, developing of an interpretive framework that is informed by African-based structures of meaning.

2. Randell Jarrell, "Review of *All God's Dangers*, by Theodore Rosengarten," *Harvard Educational Review* 45 (August 1975): 391.

3. Rosengarten, *All God's Dangers*, pp. 435–437.

4. Alfred B. Pasteur and Ivory Toldson, *Roots of Soul: The Psychology of Black Expressiveness* (Garden City, N.Y.: Anchor/Doubleday, 1982), p. 122.

5. This situation is changing as more black theologians become acquainted with historical and cultural studies of African people. A good example is Robert E. Hood, *Must God Remain Greek? Afro Cultures and God-Talk* (Minneapolis: Fortress Press, 1990).

6. Jean-Pierre Jossua, "A Crisis of the Paradigm, Or a Crisis of the Scientific Nature of Theology," in *Paradigm Change in Theology*, ed. Hans Kung and David Tracy (New York: Crossroad, 1989), pp. 256–257.

7. Cone, *God of the Oppressed*, p. 54, argues: "The form of black religious thought is expressed in the style of story and its content is liberation. Black Theology, then, is the story of black people's struggle for liberation in an extreme situation of oppression." I agree with Cone's view concerning the style of black theology. However, I have argued for a greater awareness of African cultural processes in understanding the complexity of black responses to the American situation. Liberation for the African American community has included the right to indigenous cultural expressiveness, whether it be in the form of worship or family integrity.

8. James M. Gustafson, *Can Ethics Be Christian?* (Chicago: University of Chicago Press, 1975), pp. 43–81.

POSTSCRIPT

1. Eliade, *No Souvenirs*, p. 51.

2. Archie Smith, Jr., presentation at the Conference on Ethics and Therapy in the Black Community, University of Chicago Divinity School, April 1984.

Bibliography

Achebe, Chinua. *Things Fall Apart*. New York: McDowell, Obolensky, 1959.

Andrews, William. *Sisters of the Spirit*. Bloomington: Indiana University Press, 1986.

Ansbro, John, J. *Martin Luther King, Jr.: The Making of a Mind*. Maryknoll, N.Y.: Orbis Books, 1982.

Appiah, Anthony. "Alexander Crummell and the Invention of Africa." *Massachusetts Review* 31 (1990): 385–406.

Aptheker, Herbert, ed. *The Correspondence of W. E. B. DuBois: Selections, 1877–1934*. Vol. 1. Amherst: University of Massachusetts Press, 1973.

Asante, Molefi. *The Afrocentric Idea*. Philadelphia: Temple University Press, 1981.

Baker, Houston A., Jr. "Belief, Theory, and Blues: Notes for a Post-Structuralist Criticism of Afro-American Literature." In *Studies in Black American Literature*, edited by Joe Weixlmann and Chester J. Fontenot. Vol. 2. Greenwood, Fla: Penkevill, 1986.

———. *Blues, Ideology and Afro-American Literature: A Vernacular Theory*. Chicago: University of Chicago Press, 1984.

———. *The Journey Back: Issues in Black Literature and Criticism*. Chicago: University of Chicago Press, 1980.

Baldwin, James. *The Evidence of Things Not Seen*. New York: Holt, Rinehart and Winston, 1985.

Ballanta-(Taylor), Nicholas George Julius. *Saint Helena Island Spirituals*. New York: Institute of Musical Art, 1924.

Barthes, Roland. *Mythologies*. New York: Noonday Press, 1957.

Berry, Mary Frances, and John W. Blassingame. "Africa, Slavery and the Roots of Contemporary Black Culture." In *Chant of Saints: A Gathering of Afro-American Literature, Art, and Scholarship*, edited by Michael S. Harper and Robert B. Stepto. Urbana: University of Illinois Press, 1979.

Blassingame, John W. *The Slave Community: Plantation Life in the Antebellum South*. New York: Oxford University Press, 1972.

Boas, Franz. *Race, Language and Culture*. New York: Macmillan, 1940.

Boggs, James. *Revolution and Evolution in the Twentieth Century*. New York: Monthly Review Press, 1974.

Boyd-Franklin, Nancy. *Black Families in Therapy: A Multisystems Approach*. New York: Guilford Press, 1989.

Bradley, David. *The Chaneysville Incident*. New York: Avon Books, 1981.

Brent, Linda. "Incidents in the Life of a Slave Girl." In *The Classic Slave Narratives*, edited by Henry Louis Gates Jr. New York: Mentor Books, 1987.

Comaroff, Jean. *Body of Power, Spirit of Resistance: The Culture and History of a South African People*. Chicago: University of Chicago Press, 1985.

Comstock, Gary. "Two Types of Narrative Theology." *Journal of the American Academy of Religion* 55 (Winter 1987): 687–717.

Cone, James H. *God of the Oppressed*. New York: Seabury Press, 1975.

Datrak, Ketu. *Wole Soyinka and Modern Tragedy: A Study of Dramatic Theory and Practice*. Westport, Conn.: Greenwood Press, 1986.

Davis, Angela. *Women, Race, and Class*. New York: Random House, 1981.

Douglass, Frederick. *Life and Times of Frederick Douglass: Written by Himself*. 1881. Reprint, Secaucus, N.J.: Citadel Press, 1983.

Dretzel, Hans Dieter. "On the Political Meaning of Culture." In *Beyond the Crisis*, edited by Norman Birnbaum. New York: Oxford University Press, 1977.

DuBois, W. E. B. *The Souls of Black Folk*. 1903. Reprint, New York: Bantam, 1989.

Eliade, Mircea. *No Souvenirs: Journal, 1957–1969*. New York: Harper & Row, 1977.

Eliot, T. S. "The Dry Salvages." In *Four Quartets*. 1944. Reprint, San Diego: Harvest/HBJ, 1971.

Equiano, Olaudah. "The Life of Olaudah Equiano." In *The Classic Slave Narratives*, edited by Henry Louis Gates Jr. New York: Mentor Books, 1987.

Federal Writers' Project. *Lay My Burden Down*. Chicago: University of Chicago Press, 1945.

Fernandez, James W. *Bwiti: An Ethnography of the Religious Imagination in Africa*. Princeton: Princeton University Press, 1982.

———. *Persuasions and Performances: The Play of Tropes in Culture*. Bloomington: Indiana University Press, 1986.

Fields, Margaret. "Spirit Possession in Ghana." In *Spirit Mediumship and Society in Africa*, edited by John Beattie and John Middleton. New York: Africana, 1969.

Fisher, Dexter, and Robert B. Stepto, eds. *Afro-American Literature: The Reconstruction of Instruction*. New York: Modern Language Association of America, 1979.

Fisher, Miles Mark. *Negro Slave Songs in the United States*. New York: Citadel Press, 1953.

Franklin, V. P. *Black Self-Determination: A Cultural History of the Faith of the Fathers*. Westport, Conn.: Lawrence Hill, 1984.

Frazier, E. Franklin. *The Negro Church in America*. New York: Schocken Books, 1964.

Gates, Henry Louis, Jr. *Figures in Black: Words, Signs and the "Racial" Self.* New York: Oxford University Press, 1987. 1985).

———. *The Signifying Monkey: A Theory of African-American Literary Criticism.* New York: Oxford University Press, 1988.

———. ed. " 'Race,' Writing and Difference." (special issue) *Critical Inquiry* 12 (Autumn 1985).

———. ed. *Black Literature and Literary Theory.* New York: Metheun, 1984.

———. ed. *Six Women's Slave Narratives.* New York: Oxford University Press.

Geiger, H. J. "Review of *All God's Dangers: The Life of Nate Shaw,* by Theodore Rosengarten." *The New Republic* 171 (October 12, 1974): 24.

Genovese, Eugene D. *Roll, Jordan, Roll: The World the Slaves Made.* New York: Pantheon, 1974.

Goldberg, Michael. *Theology and Narrative: A Critical Introduction.* Nashville: Abingdon Press, 1982.

Gustafson, James M. *Can Ethics Be Christian?* Chicago: University of Chicago Press, 1975.

Gutman, Herbert. *The Black Family in Slavery and Freedom, 1750–1920.* New York: Pantheon, 1976.

Hassan, I. "The Culture of Postmodernism." *Theory, Culture and Society* 2 (1985): 119–132.

Hauerwas, Stanley. *Truthfulness and Tragedy: Further Investigations into Christian Theological Ethics.* South Bend, Ind.: University of Notre Dame Press, 1977.

Hawking, Stephen. *A Brief History of Time: From the Big Bang to Black Holes.* New York: Bantam Books, 1988.

Hebdige, Dick. *Subculture: The Meaning of Style.* New York: Metheun, 1979.

Hemenway, Robert E. *Zora Neale Hurston: A Literary Biography.* Urbana: University of Illinois Press, 1977.

Henderson, Stephen. *Understanding the New Black Poetry: Black Speech and Black Music as Poetic References.* New York: Morrow, 1973.

Herskovits, Melville J. *The Myth of the Negro Past.* 1941. Reprint, Boston: Beacon Press, 1969.

Higginbotham, Evelyn Brooks. *Righteous Discontent: The Women's Movement in the Black Baptist Church, 1880–1920.* Cambridge: Harvard University Press, 1993.

Hood, Robert E. *Must God Remain Greek? Afro Cultures and God-Talk.* Minneapolis: Fortress Press, 1990.

Hurston, Zora Neale. *Mules and Men.* Bloomington: Indiana University Press, 1935.

———. *The Sanctified Church.* Berkeley: Turtle Island, 1983.

Jackson, John G. *Introduction to African Civilizations.* New York: University Books, 1970.

Jahnheinz, Jahn. *Muntu: The New African Culture.* New York: Grove Press, 1961.

Jarrell, Randall. "Review of *All God's Dangers,* by Theodore Rosengarten." *Harvard Educational Review* 45 (August 1975): 391.

Jordan, Winthrop. *White over Black: American Attitudes toward the Negro, 1550–1812.* Chapel Hill: University of North Carolina Press, 1968.

Jossua, Jean-Pierre. "A Crisis of the Paradigm, Or a Crisis of the Scientific Nature of Theology." In *Paradigm Change in Theology*, edited by Hans Kung and David Tracy. New York: Crossroad, 1989.

Joyce, Joyce A. "The Black Canon: Reconstructing Black American Literary Criticism." *New Literary History* 18 (Winter 1987): 335–344.

Jung, Carl Gustav. *Modern Man in Search of a Soul.* New York: Harcourt, Brace, 1933.

King, Martin Luther, Jr. *Stride toward Freedom: The Montgomery Story.* New York: Harper & Brothers, 1958.

King, Noel. *Religions of Africa.* New York: Harper & Row, 1970.

Levine, Lawrence W. *Black Culture and Black Consciousness: Afro-American Folk Thought from Slavery to Freedom.* New York: Oxford University Press, 1977.

Lincoln, C. Eric, and Lawrence H. Mamiya. *The Black Church in the African American Experience.* Durham: Duke University Press, 1990.

Long, Charles H. *Significations: Signs, Symbols, and Images in the Interpretation of Religion.* Philadelphia: Fortress Press, 1986.

Lovell, John Jr. *Black Song: The Forge and the Flame: How the Afro-American Spiritual Was Hammered Out.* New York: Macmillan, 1972.

MacRobert, Iain. *The Black Roots and White Racism of Early Pentecostalism in the U.S.A.* New York: St. Martin's Press, 1988.

Maduakor, Obi. *Wole Soyinka: An Introduction to His Writings.* New York: Garland, 1986.

Mathews, Donald G. *Religion in the Old South.* Chicago: University of Chicago Press, 1975.

Mays, Benjamin E. *The Negro's God as Reflected in His Literature.* 1938. Reprint, New York: Atheneum, 1968.

Mbiti, John S. *African Religions and Philosophy.* 2d ed. Oxford: Heinemann, 1989.

McClendon, James. *Biography as Theology: How Life Stories Can Remake Today's Theology.* Nashville: Abingdon Press, 1974.

McFague, Sallie. *Metaphorical Theology: Models of God in Religious Language.* Philadelphia: Fortress Press, 1982.

Meier, August, Elliot Rudwick, and Francis L. Broderick, eds. *Black Protest Thought in the Twentieth Century.* 2d ed. Indianapolis: Bobbs-Merrill, 1971.

Morrison, Toni. *Beloved.* New York: Alfred A. Knopf, 1987.

———. *The Bluest Eye.* New York: Holt, Rinehart and Winston, 1970.

———. *Song of Solomon.* New York: Alfred A. Knopf, 1977.

———. *Sula.* New York: Alfred A. Knopf, 1974.

———. *Tar Baby.* New York: Alfred A. Knopf, 1981.

Mudimbe, V. Y. *The Invention of Africa: Gnosis, Philosophy, and the Order of Knowledge.* Bloomington: Indiana University Press, 1988.

Niebuhr, H. Richard. *The Meaning of Revelation.* New York: Macmillan, 1941.

———. *The Responsible Self: An Essay in Christian Moral Philosophy.* New York: Harper & Row, 1963.

Niebuhr, Reinhold. *The Nature and Destiny of Man: A Christian Interpretation.* 2 vols. New York: Charles Scribner's Sons, 1941–1943.

Oates, Stephen B. *Let the Trumpet Sound: The Life of Martin Luther King, Jr.* New York: Mentor, 1982.

Ong, Walter J. *Orality and Literacy: The Technologizing of the Word.* New York: Routledge, 1982.

Parkin, Frank. *Max Weber.* London: Tavistock, 1982.

Parrish, Lydia. *Slave Songs of the Georgia Sea Islands.* 1942. Reprint, Athens: University of Georgia Press, 1992.

Pasteur, Alfred B., and Ivory Toldson. *Roots of Soul: The Psychology of Black Expressiveness.* Garden City, N.Y.: Anchor/Doubleday, 1982.

Poole, Fitz John Porter. "Metaphors and Maps: Towards Comparison in the Anthropology of Religion." *Journal of the American Academy of Religion* 54 (Autumn 1986): 411–457.

Puckett, Newbell Niles. *Folk Beliefs of the Southern Negro.* 1926. Reprint, Montclair, N.J.: Patterson Smith, 1968.

Raboteau, Albert J. *Slave Religion: The "Invisible Institution" in the Antebellum South.* New York: Oxford University Press, 1978.

Rampersand, Arnold. *The Art and Imagination of W. E. B. DuBois.* 2d ed. New York: Schocken Books, 1990.

Reed, Ishmael. *Mumbo Jumbo.* Garden City, N.Y.: Doubleday, 1972.

Ricoeur, Paul. "Dialogue with Paul Ricoeur." Interview by Richard Kearney. In *Dialogues with Contemporary Continental Thinkers: The Phenomenological Heritage*, edited by Richard Kearney. Manchester: Manchester University Press, 1984.

Roberts, David. "Out of Africa: The superb artwork of ancient Nubia." *Smithsonian Magazine* 24 (June 1993): 90–100.

Rosengarten, Theodore. *All God's Dangers: The Life of Nate Shaw.* New York: Avon Books, 1974.

Schreiter, Robert J. *Constructing Local Theologies.* Maryknoll, N.Y.: Orbis Books, 1985.

Segundo, Juan Luis. *The Liberation of Theology.* Maryknoll, N.Y.: Orbis Books, 1976.

Sernett, Milton C. *Black Religion and American Evangelicalism: White Protestants, Plantation Missions, and the Flowering of Negro Christianity, 1787–1865.* Metuchen, N.J.: Scarecrow Press, 1975.

Showalter, Elaine. "A Criticism of Our Own: Autonomy and Assimilation in Afro-American and Feminist Literary Theory." In *The Future of Literary Theory*, edited by Ralph Cohen. New York: Routledge, 1989.

Smith, Archie, Jr. *The Relational Self: Ethics and Therapy from a Black Church Perspective.* Nashville: Abingdon Press, 1982.

———. Presentation at the Conference on Ethics and Therapy in the Black Community. University of Chicago Divinity School, April 1984.

Smith, Theophus H. *Conjuring Culture: Biblical Formations of Black Americans.* New York: Oxford University Press, 1994.

Smitherman, Geneva. *Talkin and Testifyin: The Language of Black America.* Boston: Houghton Mifflin, 1977.

Sobel, Mechal. *Trabelin' On: The Slave Journey to an Afro-Baptist Faith.* 1979. Princeton: Princeton University Press, 1988.

Soyinka, Wole. *Art, Dialogue and Outrage: Essays on Literature and Culture.* 1988. Reprint, New York: Pantheon Books, 1993.

——. *Myth, Literature, and the African World.* New York: Cambridge University Press, 1976.

Stuckey, Sterling. *The Ideological Origins of Black Nationalism.* Boston: Beacon Press, 1972.

Thompson, Robert Farris. *Flash of the Spirit: African and Afro-American Art and Philosophy.* New York: Random House, 1983.

Thurman, Howard. *Deep River and the Negro Spiritual Speaks of Life and Death.* Richmond, Ind.: Friends United Press, 1975.

Tillich, Paul. *Systematic Theology.* 3 vols. Chicago: University of Chicago Press, 1951–1963.

——. *Theology of Culture.* London: Oxford University Press, 1959.

Toulmin, Stephen E. *Cosmopolis: The Hidden Agenda of Modernity.* New York: Free Press, 1990.

Tracy, David. *Analogical Imagination: Christian Theology and the Culture of Pluralism.* New York: Crossroad, 1981.

——. *Blessed Rage for Order: The New Pluralism in Theology.* New York: Seabury Press, 1975.

Turner, Victor. *Dramas, Fields, and Metaphors: Symbolic Action in Human Society.* Ithaca, N.Y.: Cornell University Press, 1974.

——. *The Drums of Affliction: A Study of Religious Processes among the Ndembu of Zambia.* Oxford: Clarendon Press, 1968.

——. *The Ritual Process: Structure and Anti-Structure.* Ithaca, N.Y.: Cornell University Press, 1969.

Walker, Sheila S. *Ceremonial Spirit Possession in Africa and Afro-America.* Leiden: E. J. Brill, 1972.

Walker, Wyatt T. *"Somebody's Calling My Name": Black Sacred Music and Social Change.* Valley Forge, Pa.: Judson Press, 1979.

Washington, Joseph H., Jr. *Black Sects and Cults.* Garden City, N.Y.: Anchor/Doubleday, 1973.

Werner, Craig. "New Democratic Vistas: Toward a Pluralistic Genealogy." In *Studies in Black American Literature,* edited by Joe Weixlmann and Chester J. Fontenot. Vol. 2. Greenwood, Fla: Penkevill, 1986.

White, Deborah Gray. *Ar'n't I a Woman? Female Slaves in the Plantation South.* New York: Norton, 1985.

White, Hayden. *Metahistory: The Historical Imagination in Nineteenth-Century Europe.* Baltimore: Johns Hopkins University Press, 1973.

——. *Tropics of Discourse: Essays in Cultural Criticism.* Baltimore: John Hopkins University Press, 1978.

Whitten, Norman E. and John F. Swed, eds. *Afro-American Anthropology: Contemporary Perspectives.*(New York: Free Press, 1970).

Williams, Preston. "The Ethics of Power." In *Quest for a Black Theology*, edited by James J. Gardner and J. Deotis Roberts. Philadelphia: Pilgrim Press, 1971.

Williams, Raymond. *Marxism and Literature*. New York: Oxford University Press, 1977.

Wilmore, Gayraud S. *Black Religion and Black Radicalism: An Interpretation of the Religious History of Afro-American People*. 2nd ed. Maryknoll, N.Y.: Orbis Books, 1983.

Index

DATE DUE

GAYLORD			PRINTED IN U.S.A.